The Way to Peace

The Way to Peace

MARK E. PETERSEN

BOOKCRAFT INC.
SALT LAKE CITY, UTAH
1969

2nd Printing, 1971

LITHOGRAPHED BY
PUBLISHERS PRESS

SALT LAKE CITY, UTAH
UNITED STATES OF AMERICA

Dedicated to my lovely wife
Emma Marr Petersen,
who has been a constant inspiration
to me over the years.

Contents

Foreword

Man is constantly in search of peace, not only the peace which comes with the end of wars and strife at home and abroad, but also the peace which comes with living fully the teachings of Jesus Christ, the "Prince of Peace."

In this book, *The Way to Peace,* Elder Mark E. Petersen, of the Council of the Twelve, spells out the way individuals, communities and nations can obtain such peace. His weekly editorials appearing in the Church News section of the *Deseret News* speak out frankly on day-to-day problems as they relate to those who would seek righteousness and the peace which comes from doing the will of the Lord.

For three decades these timely messages have been prepared for Latter-day Saints by one who keeps abreast of the problems of the day and who writes clearly and succinctly as he counsels the way to peace — particularly peace of mind and the enjoyment of peaceful pursuits.

Elder Petersen writes courageously and frankly on a great variety of subjects. His advice is pertinent to both young and old. He writes with a skill born of long experience in the field of journalism and he speaks forth with the authority of his position as one of the General Authorities of the Church. This combination results in timely and pertinent advice that can be accepted with confidence and trust. These inspired writings are indeed the way to peace.

—Henry A. Smith.

The Way to Peace

THE UNITED STATES is engulfed in an unfortunate war. Many say it is a war which cannot be won because of the diversified factors involved.

We call upon our enemies to halt the war, we offer concessions, we ask other nations to intercede, all to no avail.

There is no doubt about America's desire for peace. In every home there is a hope that the war may end. The ever-mounting loss of our young men is being felt nationwide.

The enemy has no apparent desire for peace, and our national leaders see no hope for an immediate end to hostilities. Some prognosticators say the war could last from 10 to 20 years. We as citizens might well remember that there is a sure way to peace, but we have stayed away from it to a large extent.

We are so absorbed in our personal — and too often selfish — pursuits and so swayed by our own "wisdom" that we have forgotten what God has said about this country and its wars. We have forgotten the promises He has made which would bring us both victory and peace, if we would but accept Him at His word.

As we cry for peace and seek the intercession of others, we also forget some of our biblical lessons about war.

In the days of Hezekiah, king of Israel, Isaiah prophesied that the Lord would not permit the Assyrians to take Jerusalem although they were besieging it with a large army. He said, "I will defend the city to save it"; and the scripture relates, "It came to pass that night that the angel of God went out and smote in the camp of the Assyrians 185,000."

Do we believe it? It was a miracle. But it happened. God is not only a God of peace, he is also a God of war when the cause is just.

In the days of Elisha, as the Syrians warred against Israel, the prophet by inspiration told the king how to array his armies and when to strike, and they were successful. At one time an entire army was taken captive. At another time, the enemy was smitten with blindness although in their worldly might they had completely surrounded the city.

That is the kind of power God will provide when his faithful believers are in a war to defend the right.

The Lord told the Prophet Joseph Smith that when his people are in jeopardy "I, the Lord, would fight their battles, and their children's battles, and their children's children's, until they had avenged themselves on all their enemies, to the third and fourth generation."

The Book of Mormon teaches (Alma 48) that if the people will serve God he will warn them when to prepare for defense and will help to fight their battles and actually deliver their enemies into their hands and give them victory.

The Book of Mormon also teaches that America is a choice land specially blessed of our Father in heaven, and that as such, He will protect it from all other nations if we will but serve Him.

We should take seriously what the prophet said:

"Behold, this is a choice land, and whatsoever nation shall possess it shall be free from bondage, and from captivity, and from all other nations under heaven, if they will but serve the God of the land, who is Jesus Christ." (Ether 2.)

What more could we hope for? Divine protection against all other nations under heaven is something which cannot be bought. It can be had only if we earn it, and to earn it we must acknowledge and serve the God of this land.

If we really want peace, are we willing to seek it in this way? Or would we prefer to trust in armed might and fight for it at the cost of thousands of lives? Even then it might be as unstable as the so-called peace we have in Korea.

During the Revolutionary War Americans learned a lesson which we should never forget. It was clearly demonstrated then that God would fulfill his word pertaining to America.

Repeatedly George Washington proclaimed his belief that our victory in that war came "by divine interposition," to use his own words.

Do we no longer remember his orders at Yorktown? Writing to his troops after the surrender of Cornwallis, he said:

"Divine service is to be performed tomorrow in the several brigades and divisions. The commander-in-chief earnestly recommends that the troops not on duty should universally attend with that seriousness of deportment and gratitude of heart which the recognition of such reiterated and astonishing interposition of Providence demands of us."

And in addressing Congress on April 30, 1789, Washington said:

"No people can be bound to acknowledge and adore the Invisible Hand which conducts the affairs of men more than the people of the United States. Every step by which they have advanced to the character of an independent nation seems to have been distinguished by some token of Providential agency." Don't we believe these things?

Lincoln virtually prayed us into victory during the Civil War. He set special days of prayer and supplication; he called his nation to repentance, and when victory came he designated days of thanksgiving to God.

It will be remembered that following the Battle of Gettysburg Lincoln visited General Sickle, who had been wounded in that battle. The general asked if the president had not been anxious about the outcome of the engagement.

"No," Lincoln replied, "I was not. Some of my cabinet and many others in Washington were, but I had no fears."

The general then asked the president what had given him this unusual assurance, to which Lincoln replied:

"Well, I will tell you how it was. In the pinch of your campaign up there, when everybody seemed panic-stricken and nobody could tell what was going to happen, oppressed by the gravity of affairs, I went to my room one day and locked the door and got down on my knees before Almighty God and prayed to Him mightily for victory at Gettysburg.

"I told Him that our cause was His cause, but that we could not stand another Fredericksburg or Chancellorsville.

"Then and there I made a solemn vow to Almighty God that if He would stand by our boys at Gettysburg

I would stand by Him. And He did stand by you boys at Gettysburg, and I will stand by Him.

"After that, and I don't know how it was, but soon a sweet comfort crept into my soul. The feeling came that God had taken the whole business into His hands, and that things would go right at Gettysburg. That is why I had no fears about you." (*Lincoln, Man of God,* by Hill.)

But Washington warned in his first inaugural address:

"We ought to be persuaded that the propitious smiles of heaven can never be expected on a nation that disregards the eternal rules of order and right which heaven itself has ordained."

If we in this nation will now repent and serve Him, and keep His laws, He will fight our battles of today, just as He did in the days of Washington and Lincoln.

America is a Christian nation. Does she believe enough in the Almighty to bring down blessings of this kind upon her armies and navies today?

Or are we so in love with our national wealth and so engrossed in the treasures it affords that we have forgotten what God can and will do if we but subject ourselves to Him?

The Almighty does live, and He is a power to be reckoned with.

Whether we choose to align ourselves with Him or not, He is there. He is all powerful, and He is ready to fight for a righteous America. He has promised that no foreign nation shall overcome us if we will but serve Him. But it cannot be a lip service!

This present war need not go on for 10 or 20 years. Our boys need not continue to die in the steaming jungles of Vietnam as they have done already by the thousands. We may have a speedy victory if we but make ourselves eligible for divine help.

The Communists are anti-Christ. America reputedly is Christian. If we are truly on the side of Christ, and since the Communists are opposed to both ourselves and the Lord, will not the Lord help us?

But we must prove ourselves by our works. It is the sacrifice of a faithful people which brings down the blessings of heaven.

Peace in Our Time?

WHY NOT RESOLVE to obtain peace this year?

It is not the kind of resolution which can be worked out at a conference table alone, although that is necessary. It is a resolution to be made in the heart of every human being, in which we shall decide that every one of us will be willing to treat everyone else as a human being, a brother in very deed.

Why not resolve to love our neighbors as ourselves? Why not so conduct ourselves that our neighbors will learn to love us?

Love does beget love, as truly as hate begets hate.

Love can conquer all. Kindness is the best panacea for our ills this world has ever known. Forgiveness is so godlike that if we are willing to exercise it we will acquire a divine characteristic which will lead the way to complete understanding. It will be as effective among us as individuals as between nations.

But that true love of mankind requires divine direction or we might err still further through our mortal weakness and thus defeat our purpose.

But such direction has been provided. It is available to all.

What is it? The Gospel of Peace which is the Gospel of Christ.

Overnight we could have peace if we were to truly live that Gospel.

"But," one will say, "most of the world is not even Christian. How can we expect them to follow a Christian plan?"

Our answer is that all nations, Christian or otherwise, have their own religions, all of which teach love of fellowmen. And furthermore, if we but set the example, it will reach the hearts of others not of our faith. Love is contagious. Regardless of race or color, all understand the universal language of kindness.

But America must take the first step. That will mean a great readjustment in our own lives. More than a third of our people are not nominal Christians, nor are they adherents to any faith. But be that as it may, they still can be influenced. But we who profess Christ must begin with ourselves.

The Christians must become TRUE Christians. They must not praise Christ with their lips, boast of their godliness, and yet live in a manner contrary to His teachings. That is hypocrisy.

If there is one thing above another that God expects of us it is sincerity.

Can we be sincere Christians if we do not serve Him and keep His commandments? Can we influence other nations to love us as they do themselves if our own lives are hypocritical, if our acts belie our professions?

America must go through a period of complete repentance. It will indeed be a major adjustment, and in many instances a complete reversal of our daily lives.

But it is the way to peace, and the ONLY way to peace. There is no other way. The wages of sin is death, and we are now rapidly learning that lesson although we refuse, in our stubbornness, to admit it.

Peace can be obtained THIS YEAR if we determine to bring it about.

In Lincoln's day the president of the United States called upon every citizen to bow himself before "the offended power" and confess both individual and national sins. He called upon them to sincerely fast and pray for forgiveness. He asked them to learn of God and serve Him.

Will today's Americans do as well?

It is admitted that in Lincoln's day, although many fasted and many prayed, it was not a universal movement. Many failed to respond to the president.

In our day the need is at least as great as in the time of Lincoln. The nation is not at war with itself — openly. But it is at war with itself beneath the surface. This war has broken out openly in scores of cities which were burned and pillaged by our own citizens. Our streets are unsafe, our college grounds even now are battle grounds in many cities. And in addition we are engaged in an Oriental conflict which could break into World War III at any moment.

If we Americans will but show enough basic character to recognize and admit our own faults, and bow before Almighty God, learn of His true Gospel, not the creeds of men, and then live that Gospel, PEACE COULD COME IN OUR TIME. It could come this very year!

But if we refuse to accept His teachings and follow His ways, peace will be taken from the earth, not to be found again until the Prince of Peace shall come, when He will destroy wickedness by divine power, which seems to be the only way mankind is willing that it be done.

Toward God or Ruin?

THE FOUNDERS OF our nation were wise men. Faced with the sternest realities of life, they were compelled to look facts squarely in the face and act accordingly. Theirs were life and death choices. They could not indulge in trivial sentimentalities.

Out of such experience these founding fathers were convinced that America cannot alienate herself from divine principles of righteousness and survive.

George Washington, our first president, was a leader in this thought. He so expressed himself repeatedly. He knew that freedom came to America by act of God, and he knew equally well that freedom would remain here only as the citizens serve God.

Said he at one time:

"We ought to be persuaded that the propitious smiles of heaven can never be expected on a nation that disregards the eternal rules of order and right which heaven itself has ordained."

Franklin spoke out even more pointedly, demanding not only faith but works as well. He denounced the tendency to put empty creeds before virtue, and reminded his fellow Americans that when we stand before the judgment bar of God "our recommendation will not be that we said, Lord, Lord, but that we did good to our fellowmen." Thoughtful leaders of American life from

Washington's day to ours have repeatedly said that to survive, America must turn to God in an earnest and sincere way. Lincoln made this almost a theme song.

Albert W. Palmer wrote in the *Christian Century*:

"Godlessness is the greatest peril of the present hour. I mean by godlessness just what the word in its barest outline means. To be godless is to be without God, to have God subtracted from you.

"To be without God is to have a world view in which there is no unifying power and no central intelligence. It is to have no moral code beyond the passing whim or temporary expediency; to live a life within which there glows no larger hope, and beneath which lies no undergirding purpose.

"It is a fundamental weakness of our age that too many people have no sense of accountability to anything beyond themselves. For them there is no Great Spirit."

Dr. Harold Lynn Hough, former president of Northwestern University, said:

"Only twice in history has there been such a moral bankruptcy as there is today. The other periods occurred at the end of the Italian Renaissance and at the end of the Roman Empire." And then he added:

"The cause of this condition is that we moderns have lost our capacity for spiritual fellowship."

The *United States News* spoke editorially on this subject and said:

"A spiritual revival would awaken America and purify her whole national life. It is not, however, to be obtained by mere expression of purpose.

"It requires action throughout our waking hours. Not until each and every one of us feels the impact of spiritual achievement, not until the eagerness to serve

God is stronger than the eagerness to serve ourselves, not until we are ready to make sacrifices of time and money and power and pride for the sake of others who need our help and guidance, will we begin to understand the elemental transformation which is requisite to the spiritual re-birth of the nation."

When General Douglas MacArthur made his V-J Day address in Tokyo Bay, he said:

"We have had our last chance. If we do not now devise some greater and more equitable system, Armageddon will be at our door. The problem basically is theological and involves a spiritual recrudescence and improvement of human character that will synchronize with our almost matchless advance in science, art, literature and all material and cultural developments of the past 2,000 years.

"It must be of the spirit if we are to save the flesh."

General Omar N. Bradley, one of the heroes of World War II, said this:

"With the monstrous weapons man already has, humanity is in danger of being trapped in this world by its moral adolescence. Our knowledge of science has clearly outstripped our capacity to control it.

"We have too many men of science; too few men of God. We have grasped the mystery of the atom and rejected the Sermon on the Mount. Man is stumbling blindly through a spiritual darkness while toying with the precarious secrets of life and death.

"The world has achieved brilliance without wisdom, power without conscience. Ours is a world of nuclear giants and ethical infants. We know more about war than we know about peace, more about killing than we know about living."

Warnings such as these have come repeatedly to Americans over the years. There has been no particular response. Still nearly half the nation belongs to no Church at all; depth of faith is not too evident among many of the others.

If America is to survive as a great nation, it must repent of its selfishness and avarice, and return to the simple truths of Christ. He can save us in this life as well as in the next. Without Him there is no salvation, either here or there.

For God And Country

ABRAHAM LINCOLN BELIEVED that the destiny of the United States is closely and intimately related to its faith in God.

He was convinced that America will be saved in any emergency if we will but serve the Almighty. But he was equally convinced that if we as a nation do not serve God, we will drift into ruin.

Said Lincoln at one time:

"My faith is greater than yours. I not only believe that Providence is not unmindful of the struggle in which this nation is engaged, that if we do not do right God will let us go our own way to ruin; and that if we do right He will lead us safely out of this wilderness, crown our arms with victory and restore our dissevered Union, as you have expressed your belief; but I also believe He will compel us to do right in order that He may do these things, not so much because we desire them, as that they accord with His plans in dealing with this nation, in the midst of which He means to establish justice.

"I think that He means that we shall do more than we have yet done in the furtherance of His plans and He will open the way for our doing it.

"I have felt His hand upon me in great trials and submitted to His guidance, and I trust that as He shall further open the way I will be ready to walk therein, relying on His help and trusting in His goodness and wisdom."

This he said in reply to a discussion with Senator James F. Wilson of Iowa.

We find ourselves in very much the same situation as did Lincoln. He was in the midst of a war in which for a long period he seemed to see no end.

For his answer, he turned to God and urged the nation to do likewise. He was sincere and humble. He acknowledged the power of Heaven in the affairs of the United States. Selfish interests in no way motivated him. He believed America has a divine destiny.

He sought only for the best interests of the country, and knew that God would help America overcome its problems if the people were only sincere.

At another time he spoke of the prayers of good Christian people seeking an end to the Civil War. He commented:

"God is on our side, and so is the Bible, and so are the churches and Christian societies and organizations — all of them, so far as I know, almost without exception.

"It makes me stronger and more confident to know that all the Christians in the loyal states are praying for our success and that all their influences are working to the same end.

"Thousands of them are fighting for us, and no one will say that an officer or a private is less brave because he is a praying soldier.

"At first, when we had such long spells of bad luck, I used to lose heart some times. Now I seem to know that Providence has protected and will protect us against any fatal defeat.

"ALL WE HAVE TO DO IS TO TRUST THE AL-
MIGHTY AND KEEP ON OBEYING HIS ORDERS
AND EXECUTING HIS WILL." (Chittenden, pp.
448-50.)

Lincoln put his finger on the problem that confronts
us today, and upon the answer to that problem.

America needs to turn to God in our present crisis,
but not in any superficial manner. Deep faith, deep conviction are what Americans need, plus a determination
to do as Lincoln said: "Keep on obeying His orders and
executing His will."

No one can say that a nation torn with internal
strife as we are now, with ever-increasing waves of
atheism, and with the drunkenness, immorality and re-
bellions that we endure, has reached that point.

America must repent and turn to God, for unless we
do, as Lincoln said, "God will let us go our own way
to ruin."

Many centuries before Lincoln, an early American
prophet said essentially the same thing:

"Behold, this is a land which is choice above all
other lands; wherefore he that doth possess it shall
serve God or shall be swept off; for it is the everlasting
decree of God." (Ether 2:10.)

Have we the courage to heed the warning before it
is too late?

The Divine Way

WHAT ARE SOME of God's rules for ending war, poverty, riots and crime?

We have tried man's ways and will continue to try them without success. But God has a plan. It is through obedience to the Gospel of the Lord Jesus Christ. And what are some of these requirements?

One of the greatest of all is the Law of the Sabbath. Moses taught that keeping the Sabbath is one of the signs by which the true believers may be identified. (Exodus 31.) Great promises have been made to all who observe this law.

But how many people now humbly worship Him on His holy day? How many use that day for pleasure and business instead?

Moses also said that recognition of a sacred Sabbath signifies the perpetual covenant existing between the Lord and His true followers. But if the sign of the covenant disappears, does the covenant itself cease to exist? Can we afford to be deprived of this covenant? Can we count the cost of such a loss?

Another of the great laws laid down by the Almighty is that pertaining to morals.

When will mankind recognize the fact that sex sin is next to murder in God's category of crime? As this world makes sex a plaything, it defies the Creator who made it and who fortified its sanctity by divine rules of conduct.

Can those who flout this law, openly or in secret, expect anything but retribution in the form of disease, destruction, and despair?

The Almighty strongly denounced the use of alcoholic beverages and enslaving stimulants. Can a generation which is willing to sell its birthright for liquor and drugs hope for blessings from the God whose word they reject?

He also requires honesty, compassion, purity and good character on the part of his followers.

Can liars, cheats, false witnesses, those who run swiftly to mischief, and those who spread discord claim the mercy of a just God? Can the dishonest? Can the unclean?

Can anything but the whirlwind come to those who deny mercy to their fellowmen, who rob widows and orphans, who are without natural affection, heady, haughty, high-minded, lovers of their own selves, covetous, boasters, blasphemers, truce breakers, false accusers, incontinent, fierce, despisers of those that are good?

Can those who refuse to do unto others as they would be done by expect the smiles of heaven? If we love not our fellowmen, as Jesus taught, then in all candor how can we profess any genuine love for God?

Can those who pray in hypocrisy, whose consciences are seared as with a hot iron, who despise true charity and mock its sacred ordinances, escape the condemnation of an indignant Deity whose Spirit will not always strive with man?

Every Christian should know that God does not walk in devious paths, nor does He condone perfidy in man. All should know too that the only path of safety is the straight and narrow way and that no one can walk therein without humbling himself before the offended

Power, acknowledging his guilt and praying for clemency as he readjusts his life.

Latter-day Saints should know by this time that all saints who keep and do His sayings, walking in obedience to the commandments, shall receive health in their navels and marrow to their bones and shall find wisdom and great treasures of knowledge, even hidden treasures, and shall find peace to their souls.

But they should also have learned by this time the truth of the Lord's words in which He said, ". . . when ye do not what I say, ye have no promise."

On the other hand, they should know that in following their leader who is their prophet and president, they can walk even through the valley of the shadow of death and fear no evil. The Almighty will lead them into green pastures and with both His staff and His rod will protect them. He will prepare a table for them even in the presence of their enemies, and goodness and mercy shall follow them all the days of their lives.

Latter-day Saints are but a small segment of the world's population, but obedience to the Lord must begin somewhere. Every Latter-day Saint, therefore, should dedicate himself to keeping the commandments of God and follow the leadership of the President of the Church. Thereby they, at least, like the leaven in the lump, will be making a good contribution to peace.

We Can Have Peace

Do HUMAN BEINGS really want peace?

We are beset on every hand with conflicts of many kinds. And all of these conflicts are of our own making.

We make our own wars, our own riots, strikes and lock-outs, and we sow our own seeds of family strife. We drink ourselves into alcoholism and drive ourselves into insanity and death with illicit drugs. At the same time we invite a tidal wave of social disease by our own immoral practices. We are the creators of our own miseries.

But if we would, we could avoid them all, so easily and so simply. It could be done this very day, and thus we could change the world from a state bordering on despair, to one of happiness — if we only would.

Every person on earth really yearns for peace. The starving would like more food, the homeless seek shelter. Those who mourn the loss of loved ones on the battle field pine for comfort to their souls, and indulge in what seems to be a forlorn hope that carnage may cease and that swords may be beaten into plowshares.

All profess to want peace, but how few will take the steps to obtain it!

Basically, wars, crime, and sin in general, are the products of selfishness. As long as this condition persists, conflicts will continue in the world.

But there is a cure for it — a way to end it forever. It is found in the Gospel of Christ.

If we loved our neighbors as ourselves we would begin to wipe out selfishness. If we were to do unto others as we would be done by, we would uproot the greed, the avarice, the stubbornness and the dictatorial tendencies that break up homes, induce divorce, spawn crime and foster immorality.

If we were to "turn the other cheek" as offenses come, if we were to reconcile all our differences before we approach the altar of God as the Savior said, if we refrained from anger and gossip, from unwise judgments and from considering other people as fools, we would lay a foundation of mutual understanding even with our enemies.

If we would forgive as we seek forgiveness for ourselves, if we would be merciful and kind and long-suffering, patient and helpful, a new day would dawn for us all and we would begin to learn what the angels meant as they sang on that first Christmas night.

Good will? What does it mean? Can it be something superficial — just on the surface? Can it exist without sincerity, humility, and purity of motives?

There is no place for hypocrisy in good will. There is room only for the Golden Rule.

And if we do not live that law we never can have good will nor peace on earth nor love among our fellowmen.

Christ offers us the good and abundant life. It would be a life so good that all the ills of the present day would disappear.

That life would be so abundant that everyone would enjoy the riches of the earth, yes, all the things that make for comfort and prosperous living.

And this may be achieved simply by overcoming self and following the pathway of the Babe of Bethlehem.

It was no idle song the angels sang that night. It was full of meaning and had great significance. It was God's offer to the world and to all mankind of

> Peace on earth,
> Good will to men.

The Peace That Is Not Here

THERE IS CONFLICT in the place where Christ was born. Shots have broken the stillness of the air about Bethlehem. Battlements are nearby. Armed patrols keep down the threat of rioting. There is no peace where the Prince of Peace was born.

But neither is there real peace anywhere else. War in Vietnam goes on. The entire Far East is caught up in a series of confrontations in which thousands die, many of them innocent bystanders. There is a constant struggle for power and dominion.

In our country what do we have? On the surface there are many peaceful pursuits. Children play unharmed, in schools they are taught their lessons; people attend church services, and go to their daily employment. For the most part there is apparent peace in our land.

But under the surface there are stresses and strains which could result in an insurrection. There are threats of war as those who foment riots and arson talk of "getting guns" and taking by force whatever their whims dictate.

There is widespread labor strife. Long and costly strikes sap the vitality of industry, even interfering with delivery of supplies to our armies in Vietnam. Political campaigns become sources of costly conflict, dividing large factions against others, not in clean competition, but in bitterness and hate which, if allowed to increase, could threaten the safety of the nation.

There is also a dreadful rise in crime which gives anything but peace to the populace at large, and costs the nations billions of dollars every year, not to mention the lives and human suffering which are involved.

Where is peace? Do we really want it? And if we do, how much are we willing to give for it? Can it be purchased with money or favors? Can it be compared to commodities in the market place?

Can it even be found in parliaments or congresses or conventions or synods?

Where is peace, and how may we obtain it? All right-thinking people desire it, but few seem to be willing or know how to take the necessary steps to acquire it.

Where is peace? It is to be found only with the Prince of Peace. He has given us the formula by which all mankind may become a true brotherhood, and through which all of man's antagonism toward one another may be erased.

There was deep meaning in the first Christmas song of the angels: "Peace on earth, good will to men." That is what Christ can bring. It is what He came to bring. It is what He holds out to everyone.

Peace, holy peace. Peace of mind, peace in the soul. The peace which passeth all understanding!

Some feel that it is something to be obtained only in heaven, not to be enjoyed on this side of eternity. But that is not the Lord's plan. He intends that we shall have peace here and now. He gave us the formula by which we may obtain it. The formula is effective. It never fails. The failure is in our own refusal to use it.

And what is that formula? It is the simple Gospel of the Lord Jesus Christ, which teaches mankind to be true brethren and sisters, to love our neighbors as ourselves, to go the extra mile, to turn the other cheek, to forgive — even seventy times seven — to do unto others as we would be done by, to seek reconciliation wherein we have offended others, to avoid judging others, that we ourselves may not be judged; to be kind, patient, long-suffering, charitable, temperate, humble and God-like.

This is the formula. If we were to follow it, wars would end, there would be no rioting, pillaging, or assaults. Crime would disappear completely.

Every man would be a friend to his neighbor, every woman would be an angel of mercy. Children would grow up in an atmosphere of righteousness. No one would set them bad examples, none would teach them to sin.

Governments would be run honestly, nations would not learn war any more.

Wracked as we are with man-made strife and suffering, is it not time now to turn to God? Have we not adequately proven to ourselves what life must be when we reject the divine plan?

Are we to remain so blind and so stubborn that we will refuse to acknowledge our mistakes and humbly turn to the only source of true joy and happiness?

Need we "save face" in the midst of the morass in which we have placed ourselves? Shall we not be willing to repent now and humble ourselves before the Almighty, turn to Him and accept His unfailing way to peace?

Christ is the Prince of Peace. It is His formula of which we speak. It is His gospel, so long neglected. It is here for us all — freely given.

"Come unto me," He says, "all ye that labour and are heavy laden, and I will give you rest. Take my yoke upon you, and learn of me, for I am meek and lowly in heart, and ye shall find rest unto your souls. For my yoke is easy, and my burden is light."

Our Debt To "Honest Abe"

AMERICA'S GREAT MEN have left us an invaluable heritage.

Greatness does not appear frequently — that is, the greatness which leaves an indelible righteous stamp upon the world — but when it does it invariably points to the divine destiny which God has provided for mankind.

Abraham Lincoln was of that stature.

Lincoln was one of the great men of all time, of all nations. Around the world he is quoted. Around the world he is honored. Everywhere he is recognized as a specially endowed figure whose influence still spreads a light of hope in a benighted world.

What did Lincoln give to us — and what do we and mankind in general owe Lincoln?

In the first place Lincoln was a man of God. He had a simple, childlike faith, such as that spoken of by the Savior.

When he cried out in prayer, it was with an undoubting trust. He knew God was a living presence; he knew the Almighty was his Father who had raised him up for a special mission. All of this he attested to. None did he ever deny.

"He prayed as if everything depended upon God; he worked as if everything depended upon himself," as John Wesley Hill expressed it when he also said:

"He seemed to be of the same fibre with the prophets of Holy Writ, combining the kingly and priestly functions essential to the service of his nation and time."

At one time Lincoln wrote:

"That the Almighty does make use of human agencies and directly intervenes in human affairs is one of the plainest statements in the Bible. I have had so many evidences of his direction, so many instances when I have been controlled by some power other than my own will, that I cannot doubt that this power comes from above. I am satisfied that when the Almighty wants me to do, or not to do, a particular thing, He finds a way of letting me know it."

Lincoln — as a citizen of the world — set us an example of childlike faith in God, utterly and completely at variance with the so-called "intellectual" criticism of God and the Bible so rampant in the world today.

Lincoln knew that our country's safety depends upon our obedience to God — he said it in so many words — and also that when we abandon the Almighty our country is lost, and we are lost with it.

What do we owe Lincoln? We owe it to him — and to our country — and to our God — to cherish the kind of faith he held so dear, and to be as willing as he to bow to the will of an over-ruling Providence.

Lincoln was honest. For us of today, "honest" is part of his name. There was only one "honest Abe" in the world, and whenever that expression is used, we think only of Lincoln.

How could Lincoln be the spiritual giant that he was without this quality of honesty? He left us a heritage of honest principles. If we now build on that honesty, we shall continue to be great as a nation. But if we relinquish it, we shall slip into the abyss of destruction.

What do we owe Lincoln? We owe him our willingness to preserve the type of integrity which he willed to this nation. It was through it he saved our country. It is only through it that we of today can save our land.

Integrity in public office —

Integrity in the home —

Integrity in the individual heart —

These are the bequests left us by Lincoln.

Our performance in integrity is a debt we owe to Lincoln and to all mankind.

Sum up all of his accomplishments — the preservation of the nation, freeing the slaves, his kindness and mercy to the unfortunate, his compassion for his soldiers, his statesmanship at the head of government — and all will be seen as but products of his two outstanding characteristics: his spirituality and his uncompromising honesty.

We owe it to Lincoln, we owe it to our nation, to each other and to ourselves, to enthrone those same attributes within our souls and thus perpetuate the depth of character without which we can never survive as a nation, nor be happy as individuals.

Our Debt To Washington

As our nation was saved through the divine strength and inspiration which came to Abraham Lincoln, so it was founded in the first place by the aid of heaven and the deep spiritual nature of George Washington.

Anyone reading the colonial history of the United States must know that our country was established by the direct intervention of heaven. They must know too that men like Washington, Franklin, Adams and Hancock depended upon the Almighty, and that when Jefferson wrote into the Declaration of Independence the words, "With a firm reliance on the protection of Divine Providence," he expressed the faith of the entire thirteen colonies.

When Washington fought, he did so with trust in God. He did not take up arms, nor the command of his soldiers, until he had gone to the Almighty in earnest prayer.

There was hardly a battle fought that was not preceded by appeals to Deity. There was never a victory won but was followed by an acknowledgement of divine aid.

This heaven-sent assistance was a great reality to Washington. He knew the weakness of his armies, their handicaps, their poor equipment and the strength of the well-trained Redcoats who faced him. And when victory came — almost as a gift — Washington was the first to acknowledge it.

America should ever remember his statement after the battle of Yorktown:

"Divine service is to be performed tomorrow in the several brigades and divisions. The commander-in-chief earnestly recommends that the troops not on duty should universally attend with that seriousness of deportment and gratitude of heart which the recognition of such reiterated and astonishing interposition of providence demands of us."

This is characteristic of his repeated statements on the subject. God was the moving factor in his life. Washington knew of the divine existence. He knew too that the Almighty had fought for the colonists, giving them liberty.

Students of the Book of Mormon are well aware of the extent to which Deity did take part in that war. The vision of the first Nephi clearly predicted that God would win the war for the colonists, and the words of the Savior are so clear that none can misunderstand:

"It is wisdom in the Father that they [the Gentiles in America] should be established in this land and be set up as a free people by the power of the Father, that these things might come forth from them unto a remnant of your seed, that the covenant of the Father may be fulfilled which he hath covenanted with his people, O house of Israel." (3 Nephi 21:4.)

The hand of oppression had to be removed from America. The people who lived here must be set up as a free people. IT WAS DONE BY ACT OF THE FATHER. But a human agent was required as in all other things. Washington was an agent of heaven in bringing about His work. He realized it, and knew that God was fighting his battles for him. So in humility and gratitude he thanked heaven repeatedly for it.

Why was America set up as a free nation? In the words of the Savior, "that these things [meaning the

Gospel as recorded in the Book of Mormon] might come forth from them [the Gentiles in America who set up the nation] unto a remnant of your seed [the descendants of Lehi] that the covenant of the Father may be fulfilled which he hath covenanted with his people, O house of Israel."

Thus we see Washington in his true perspective.

As a man of God he was raised up to be the agent through whom the battles of freedom would be fought, and whom God would assist in obtaining the victory.

He was an agent, too, in assisting to set up the new government after the war, and was the first president of this free land.

What do we owe Washington?

We owe it to him to perpetuate what he began, a free nation, under God, to remain free that "these things" (the divine message of the Restored Gospel) might go abroad in fulfillment of the divine covenant.

In the words of the Prophet Joseph Smith: "Brethren, shall we not go on in so great a cause? Go forward, and not backward. Courage, brethren, and on, on to victory!"

Perilous Times Shall Come

MANY PROPHECIES RELATE to the last days. One of the most descriptive of them all is Paul's prediction to Timothy when he said:

"In the last days perilous times shall come. For men shall be lovers of their own selves . . . lovers of pleasures more than lovers of God. Having a form of godliness but denying the power thereof." (2 Tim. 3:1-2, 4-5.)

It goes without saying that there are millions of good people in the world, Christians and non-Christians alike, who devotedly serve their God as far as their knowledge will permit. They possess much of the "milk of human kindness" and could hardly be included within the scope of Paul's prediction.

But obviously he envisioned enough of the world's population to whom his description does apply to characterize a significant portion of this generation.

Examine his words. He makes three points, and since he describes conditions related to the times in which we live, we should be keenly aware of what he says.

He wrote of our generation:

1 — Men shall be lovers of their own selves.

2 — They shall be lovers of pleasure more than lovers of God.

3 — They shall have a form of godliness but deny the power thereof.

Consider each for a moment.

What does it mean to be "lovers of our selves"? In short it simply means to be selfish — self-centered and self-seeking.

And what does all this selfishness lead to? All the evils of life: crime, immorality, divorce, unkindness, dishonesty, avarice, pleasure-seeking, war — in fact the whole list of offenses involved in man's inhumanity to man.

Selfishness is one of the main reasons why some love pleasure more than God, and why they are content with a form of godliness while denying the power thereof.

It is what makes people want to "have their cake and eat it too," to use a much worn but descriptive expression. They want to "straddle the fence." They endeavor to serve two contrary masters at the same time, hoping in their selfishness to get gain from both.

They seek to palliate their religious consciences with a form of godliness and still enjoy the worldly things. This is why their hearts are far from the Lord since they are more interested in self-aggrandizement than anything else.

They deny the power of godliness because it is the antithesis of selfishness. It teaches men to do unto others as they would be done by, to love their neighbors as themselves, to be "Good Samaritans," to go the extra mile, to give their coat and their cloak as well, to be peacemakers, merciful, just, kind and forgiving.

Commenting on the fact that selfishness now costs America nearly thirty billion dollars a year in crime alone, J. Edgar Hoover, the great head of the FBI, recently said:

"What a grim and unhappy commentary on the moral climate of this great nation! The moral strength of our country has decreased alarmingly.

"We must return to the teachings of God if we are to cure this sickness. These shocking statistics, together with the public's apparent indifference to them, are indicative of the false morality we are tolerating today.

"It is a false code which is based on the worship of things of man's own creation. It is as imperfect and feeble as man himself.

"However captivating to the senses, this type of moral climate cannot give the support nor the strength which is so vital to our national survival.

"This breakdown in our moral standards can only render us impotent as a people and as a nation."

Speaking of the selfishness which breaks up homes, President David O. McKay once said:

"A married woman who refuses to assume the responsibility of motherhood, or who, having children, neglects them for pleasure or social prestige, is recreant to the highest calling and privilege of womanhood.

"The father, who, because of business or political responsibilities, fails to share with his wife the responsibilities of rearing his sons and daughters, is untrue to his marital obligations, is a negative element in what might and should be a joyous home atmosphere, and is a possible contributor to discord and delinquency."

When we become lovers of our own selves we undermine the very foundations on which we stand. We build in ourselves a false sense of security.

What Great Men Say

MAN CANNOT LIVE happily without God. There is only one way to happiness in this life, and that is through acceptance of God's teachings.

All great men — the deep thinkers — of the world agree on this point. God is so important in the lives of the truly great that Voltaire once said that if there were no God we would have to invent one.

The great need of the world today is an acceptance of the Almighty, with a willingness to serve Him. Without Him, our crises will continue to grow, our misunderstandings will increase, nation will continue to oppose nation, individuals will never cease to harbor hate and selfishness.

General Douglas MacArthur said a significant thing in his V-J Day address in Tokyo. As he surveyed the results of World War II, he said:

"We have had our last chance. If we do not now devise some greater and more equitable system, Armageddon will be at our door. The problem basically is theological, and involves a spiritual recrudescence and improvement of human character that will synchronize with our almost matchless advance in science, art, literature and all material and cultural developments of the past 2,000 years. It must be of the spirit if we are to save the flesh."

It is remarkable that others of our national leaders have expressed this identical thought in terms just as unmistakable.

Daniel Webster in 1852 said:

"If we and our posterity shall be true to the Christian religion, if we and they shall live always in the fear of God and shall respect his commandments, if we and they shall maintain just moral sentiments and such conscientious convictions of duty as shall control the heart and life, we may have the highest hopes of the future fortunes of our country, and we may be sure of one thing: our country will go on prospering.

"But if we and our posterity reject religious instruction and authority, violate the rules of eternal justice, trifle with the injunctions of morality and recklessly destroy the political Constitution which holds us together, no one can tell how sudden a catastrophe may overwhelm us, that shall bury all our glory in profound obscurity."

And J. Edgar Hoover, our great head of the FBI, said:

"What we need in America today is a return to the God of our Fathers and a most vigorous defense against the minions of godlessness and atheism."

Many other quotations might be given from many other leaders. They would all say essentially the same thing: America needs to return to God.

The riots, strikes, anarchy, arson, thievery, attacks upon the person, murders, rapes, neglect of parents, and the waywardness of youth all attest to our departure from a true worship of the Almighty.

No one who really believes in Christ would offend his neighbor.

No one who worships God with a sincere heart would rise up against law and order, and pillage, burn and steal.

No one who is converted to the Gospel of Christ would be guilty of crime, assault or immorality.

The widespread lawlessness which has marked our land, and which is seen in nearly every other land, is but evidence of the apostasy from or the disregard for the basic spiritual qualities which should mark a true civilization.

As Woodrow Wilson so effectively said in his day:

"The sum of the whole matter is this — that our civilization cannot survive materially unless it be redeemed spiritually. It can only be saved by becoming permeated with the Spirit of Christ and being made free and happy by practices which spring out of that Spirit."

Our Nation's Flag

ONCE A YEAR we set aside a day which we call "Flag Day." It is noticed by comparatively few people. Some fly their national emblem, but most do not. Many in fact do not so much as own a flag to fly.

But the flag is significant.

In the days of the ancient Nephite armies, Captain Moroni raised a flag to his people. They were at war. Their enemies were upon them from the outside, while from the inside traitors sought to destroy the freedom of the people, not only to erase liberty in government and set up a dictatorship but also to make the nation more than ever vulnerable to enemy attacks from without.

Moroni rallied his people to the flag for a two-fold purpose: One was to preserve their liberties at home and avoid enslavement.

The other was to stir up the people to fight against outside armies seeking their destruction.

He succeeded in both. He saved their liberty, putting down the traitors within, and fought to victory against invading armies from the outside.

In our own country, our leaders have done similar things. Washington was like Moroni in that he rallied loyalties at home and defeated enemies from abroad.

Lincoln, too, was like Moroni, for he also united people under one flag, while resisting an enemy from without which would have taken advantage of a divided nation, weak from its battle wounds.

We need a Moroni today. But we need not only one, we need millions — brave men and women who will stand up for the principles represented in their flag, and be willing if necessary to give their lives in its defense.

Today, as in the days of Moroni, we are under attack from two sides. From the inside we are subverted by traitors who would destroy our freedom in subtle ways. From without are the Red forces which would destroy that same freedom in their own vicious manner.

Only a united citizenry can defeat these enemies. Only harmonious action can provide the strength that is necessary under existing circumstances.

We must protect our rights as citizens. They are divine. We are granted free agency by the Almighty, who also gave us our free constitutional government to protect those rights. These too we must defend.

And we must be willing to unite under one banner — Old Glory — in unbroken resistance to communistic powers which would wipe us off the face of the earth if they dared. They have the weapons to do so, and they know it. They hesitate only from fear of our own more powerful arsenals.

But as Lincoln said, fire power will not save our nation. Our salvation must arise from the hearts of the citizenry.

And the hearts of the citizenry, to be successful, must have in them something other than hatred of the enemy, or than selfishness to preserve our easy way of life. They must be filled with the fire of Patrick Henry. They must be blessed with the divine faith of Washington, the mercy of Lincoln, and the full acceptance of the Lord Jesus Christ as the God of this land.

When we realize that the forces opposing us, both within and without, are anti-Christ in their purposes, we must recognize that this is no time for us to default to the enemy or give him aid or abet his efforts by allowing our faith in Christ to falter. This is no time to deny the Savior or doubt His divinity as many now do. This is no time to join the modern trend in saying that God is dead.

This should be a day of faith, of rededication to the Lord Jesus Christ and all His righteous principles. This should be a day to remember that His Gospel is the perfect law of liberty, and if we hope to preserve our liberty, there is only one way — and that is obedience to the perfect law upon which freedom is based.

Ours is a Christian nation. It is dedicated to the principles of justice and liberty for all. Its founders were devout, God-fearing men. Through the inspiration which came to them they provided for us a government based upon divine principles, for although they did not realize it, they were raised up by the Almighty for that very purpose.

And those men adopted a flag to represent their ideals and the sacred principles of their hard-won liberty.

That flag was the Stars and Stripes.

To them it stood for all that they had put into the founding of this new republic. To them it represented freedom, justice, and equal rights for all. To them it meant a government of, by and for the people. It meant an answer to their prayers, earnest, heart-felt prayers which had accompanied every effort in the founding of this republic.

And it meant that Divine Providence watches over America!

The flag should mean nothing less to us of today. If we do not so accept it, we should readjust our thinking, and learn what genuine Americanism really is.

A Deep Source Of Comfort

THOUGHTFUL AMERICANS ARE alarmed over the "state of the nation" at the present time. Many conditions add to their fears.

In spite of reports of victories in Vietnam, the over-all situation in Asia becomes more gloomy by the day. Hopes of peace are indeed fleeting, to say the least.

At home the constant recurrence of riots strikes fear to the hearts of peaceful citizens, making them wonder to what extent anarchy will continue to be permitted and how far it will go toward supplanting law and order.

The constant and shocking rise in crime is most disturbing, particularly so as courts become more lenient and enforcement measures weaken.

Labor strife becomes ever more vexing. It shows in stark relief how industrial strikes could completely cripple the nation and how, under some circumstances, they could even become tools in the hands of ruthless leaders of Communist-infiltrated organizations to leave us helpless in an enemy take-over.

Some of our substantial citizens actually fear for the future of our nation, and with good cause.

But there is comfort in the prophecies of the scriptures pertaining to this land.

In the first place, America is a nation of divinely appointed destiny, and that destiny has not yet been fulfilled. It is not a political destiny as most people think. It is a destiny closely related to the work of the Restored Gospel of the Lord Jesus Christ.

The Savior told the ancient Nephites about modern America, and explained to them that we — as a nation of "Gentiles" — would be raised up as a free people by the act of the Father for a particular purpose. That purpose was for the propagation of the Restored Gospel.

The work of the Church is far from finished. In fact, it is hardly getting a good start. Most of the growth of the Church is yet in the future. It will therefore require the continued protecting power of the "Gentile nation" set up to provide the necessary free agency, free press, freedom of worship and assembly, not to mention the international influence which will protect American missionaries in their world-wide proselyting effort.

But there is still another important prophecy which is vital to us.

Readers of the Book of Mormon are familiar with it:

"And he had sworn in his wrath unto the brother of Jared, that whoso should possess this land of promise, from that time forth and forever, should serve him, the true and only God, or they should be swept off.

"And this cometh unto you, O ye Gentiles, that ye may know the decrees of God — that ye may repent, and not continue in your iniquities until the fulness come, that ye may not bring down the fulness of the wrath of God upon you as the inhabitants of the land have hitherto done.

"Behold, this is a choice land, and whatsoever nation shall possess it shall be free from bondage, and from captivity, and from all other nations under heaven, IF

THEY WILL BUT SERVE THE GOD OF THE LAND, WHO IS JESUS CHRIST."

Recent statistics are most encouraging and comforting to all who believe in that prophecy.

There are more professed Christians in the United States today than ever before in history. The increase in Christian church membership is rising faster than at any previous time.

In 1935, for example, only 41 per cent of the total United States population was enrolled in Christian denominations. In 1945 the percentage had jumped to 50, and the religious census of 1965 revealed that the percentage had gone up to 64.4. Furthermore the Gallup survey of a few months ago showed that 45 per cent of the entire adult population of America attends religious services every Sunday. More than 90 per cent of the population say they believe there is a God.

A recent report of the *U.S. News and World Report* indicates that only 31 per cent of all members of Christian denominations in America NEVER go to church. The remaining 69 per cent attends more or less regularly.

Another most encouraging factor is that the United States is the most productive missionary field in the world for the Latter-day Saints. More people join the Church in America than anywhere else, and more baptisms per missionary are recorded in the United States than anywhere.

In spite of war and riots, crime and widespread irresponsibility, the faith of Christ is increasing in America. What a contrast to other countries where church attendance as shown in a national survey is down to 10 per cent in some nations, and as low as 5 per cent in others!

The safety of America lies in acceptance of Jesus Christ. Preaching and living the Gospel is the surest defense of this nation. Enemies may rage, both within and without, but if the majority of Americans will continue to accept Christ and serve him to the best of their knowledge, he will protect them and preserve our nation.

Hysteria Vs. Common Sense

RECENT MONTHS HAVE cast a shadow of gloom and despair over some parts of the United States as wholesale lawlessness has erupted into riots and mobbings.

It has reached a point in some cities where peace-loving people no longer feel safe on the streets, in public parks, or even on school grounds.

Some of the most regrettable blotches on the American scene have occurred among students at our public schools and colleges.

They have occurred in varying degrees. Some students persecute others for trivial personal reasons, and organize "cutting" acts which are cruel in the extreme.

Many students have felt, because of a growing sense of mistaken freedom, that they must be against something or everything and that the best way to express this attitude is to join riots or strikes or indulge in their own peculiar brand of "sanctions."

Student riots are among the most difficult of all for sober-minded people to understand. Students are presumably in school for learning and developing wisdom which will assist them in their future lives.

But when they cast common sense aside and participate in the hysteria of rioting, they throw to the winds all their acquired culture and all regard for the very system which provides the education they supposedly seek.

Ask many of these students why they participated in riots, and they frankly admit they do not know. "Everyone was doing it" is their most logical response. Is there any intelligence in that?

Too often it is to become part of the crowd, so they think. But frequently these so-called "crowds" are gangs led and inspired by foreign elements, trying to overthrow our government. Yet, many follow them, thoughtlessly and foolishly, much to their subsequent regret.

No one has the right to destroy another's property. No one has a right to assault another individual.

Resorting to violence is the way of the jungle, not the path of civilized and supposedly cultured persons.

Latter-day Saints must be ever law-abiding. Devoted members of the Church can never participate in any form of rioting or violence, gang fights, or resistance to law enforcement officers.

Latter-day Saints are committed to the principle of honoring, upholding and sustaining the law, and as such must forever shun unlawful acts.

It is as much a part of our religion to accept that principle as it is to believe in faith, repentance and baptism.

Lawlessness is opposed to the teachings of the Savior. It is stark disobedience. It is destructive and leads to anarchy and chaos.

Our religion teaches that the Constitution of the United States is an inspired document, guaranteeing freedom and protection to every person.

Therefore we must sustain that document, and the rights it gives us to life, liberty and the pursuit of happiness.

Those rights provide for peaceful assembly, not riots and bloodshed.

They are to establish order and tranquillity in our communities, not gang fights leading to destruction of life, limb and property.

They provide due process of law to settle differences, not taking the law into our own hands.

Our nation is built upon observance of law and order and our Church rests upon the same principle.

If, as Christians, we are able to accept the teachings of Christ, most certainly we must follow His example, do unto others as we would be done by, and uphold the righteous principles which guarantee our happiness.

Would Jesus be our Savior today if He had instigated riots and insurrection against Herod and Pilate?

Would we worship Him as we now do if He had been a rabble-rouser, inciting open rebellion?

Then can we say we follow Him if we resort to mob hysteria now and riot, burn and kill?

Without consistency of conduct there is no true Christianity. Latter-day Saints must constantly and consistently obey the law.

Honesty Is Basic

HONESTY IS ONE of the most important tenets of our religion, and one of the most difficult to live for most people.

Yet it is as fundamental to true Christianity as baptism, faith or repentance. It is the foundation of all character development.

As no man can see the kingdom of heaven without baptism, as explained by the Savior, neither can anyone see that sacred place without honesty.

Our Christian civilization is built upon integrity. Without it our way of life would collapse.

If we allow dishonesty to weave itself into the fabric of our lives, we invite moral suicide.

Dishonesty in the world is appalling, both in petty and major crime, and yet we claim to be a Christian nation.

Can we convince ourselves that we are Christian if Christian ideals are not practiced in our daily lives? No professed Christian can be a Christian indeed if he is not honest.

To profess belief in Christ, and yet refuse to live His laws, is apostasy from Christ to the extent of our disobedience.

No one can separate the Christian life from the Christian religion, and there can be no Christian life without honesty.

Faith without works is as dead in this regard as in any other. The Savior is strict in His requirement that we keep His commandments.

And yet He is most gracious in His kindly invitation to help us overcome our evil tendencies. He said: "Come unto me, all ye that labor and are heavy laden, and I will give you rest. Take my yoke upon you, and learn of me; for I am meek and lowly in heart: and ye shall find rest unto your souls."

But can rest come to the insincere? Can they have peace of mind? They can if they change their ways and repent, but not otherwise.

Honesty is intimately and inseparably related to true charity.

Charity is the perfect love of Christ.

Can there be true charity, then, without honesty?

Is there any charity in a dishonest act?

> Though I speak with the tongues of men and of angels and have not honesty, I am become as sounding brass or a tinkling cymbal.

How is a man profited if by dishonorable means he shall gain the whole world, but lose his own soul?

What shall a man give in exchange for his soul?

It is unthinkable that anyone would hide under a cloak of piety while deceiving his fellowmen, yet it is done.

Paul once asked the Corinthians if Christ is divided.

Can He be divided on any matter of principle?

Does He deal in double standards?

Does He countenance devious practices?

Is there any duplicity in Him?

Then can duplicity exist in His followers?

What does He mean when He says:

Thou shalt not lie
Thou shalt not steal
Thou shalt not covet
Thou shalt not bear false witness?

Does He give us permission to tell little lies with the understanding that we will not tell big ones?

Does He allow us to steal a little here and a little there, providing we do not commit grand larceny?

The Book of Mormon speaks of the power of the devil in the latter days and tells of his persuasive efforts to cheat and deceive human beings.

The scripture says he will cause anger to rage in the hearts of some, but others "will he pacify, and lull them away into carnal security, [so] that they will say: All is well in Zion; yea, Zion prospereth, all is well — and thus the devil cheateth their souls, and leadeth them away carefully down to hell.

"And behold, others he flattereth away, and telleth them there is no hell; and he saith unto them: I am no devil, for there is none — and thus he whispereth in their ears, until he grasps them with his awful chains, from whence there is no deliverance." (2 Nephi 28: 21-22.)

Lucifer also urges us to "eat, drink, and be merry," saying "it shall be well with us . . . Eat, drink, and be merry; nevertheless, fear God — he will justify in committing a little sin; yea, lie a little, take advantage of one because of his words, dig a pit for thy neighbor; there is no harm in all this; and do all these things, for tomorrow we die; and if it so be that we are guilty, God will beat us with a few stripes, and at last we shall be saved in the kingdom of God." (2 Nephi 28:7-8.)

What a pity that many people actually believe that devilish doctrine!

With false teachings such as those Lucifer induces many to cross the line into his realm, persuading them that they can in fact serve two opposing masters and get gain from both.

But there is only one God, and only one way to be saved in His presence. That is by avoiding all forms of hypocrisy and by honestly and sincerely keeping His commandments.

Our Changing World

CONDITIONS IN THE world are changing so rapidly that it is difficult to keep up with them.

It is said that the reservoir of available knowledge is doubling every nine or ten years, and with this new knowledge comes a flow of new discoveries, new devices and new horizons.

We send men to the moon and are thrilled with their exploits, looking forward expectantly to their further projects. We take pictures of the earth from outer space, and send television cameras to Mars and obtain pictures in return, publishing them in our daily newspapers.

We use computers to run our businesses, aid our schools and do our genealogical work. Our medical men have extended our longevity.

The "horse and buggy days" are not even known to most of our population, the average age of which is now down to about 27 years. Only a small segment of our population can remember when there were no radios.

And who, a generation ago, would have thought that a white shirt could be made from a piece of coal, or oil from shale rocks on the mountain side? And which of our grandparents could have guessed that the kerosene in their lamps which so dimly lighted their homes, would ever be used to power the mighty jet airplanes of today? It is a fast-changing world indeed.

But there are some things which never change, and never will. There is a divine constancy in the world. There is the reminder that God never changes, nor do His laws, and that such basics as high morals and good character never can be altered by any of man's intellectual or physical advances.

All the computers and space ships we can possibly make will never alter the principle of honesty. No scientific marvel of this or any age can change the ugly face of unchastity.

We take pride in our space exploits, and justly so, but let us never forget that it was God who made space and that He and His angels have been space travelers for eternities.

We marvel at the intricacies of our computers in solving mathematical and other problems, but let us not forget that we know very little about the wonders of the universe which are so intricate that even Einstein felt that our knowledge is but a faint reflection of the infinity of God.

We are now only beginning to learn smatterings of what the Lord has done. He made the worlds and the laws which govern them. And He made them for a specific purpose — the advancement of mankind.

But knowing that all advancement is not found in the realm of the intellect, and to further the same purpose for which He made the universe, He laid down moral laws to aid man toward his ultimate destiny, that of becoming like our Father in heaven.

It takes more than scientific achievements, dazzling as they are, to make us God-like. Without goodness — in character, in Christ-like living, and in clean morals — it can never be.

Artificiality characterizes much of man's world today, together with a refusal to face certain basic facts. Hypocrisy is a crying evil.

It is possible that our scientific progress can fail through a breakdown in character. All of our vaunted intellectuality can fade and die in the ashes of moral corruption.

In the whirl of present-day change, we must keep our feet on the ground and maintain our proper balance. We must not build on the sand.

We must admit that artificiality, dishonesty and hypocrisy can destroy us, and that immorality is an affront to God. It is filth carried to the nth degree. It can decimate the race.

Irreligion has a deadly effect on individuals and nations. Atheism is suicidal. Permissiveness as we know it is self-destructive.

The Almighty said that in these latter days conditions would be as they were in the days of Noah, when to wipe out corruption, God spared only eight persons from the flood.

By their Babylonic sins many in the world are rejecting God today. They seem not to have the intelligence or the wisdom, even in this time of great achievements, to understand that the certain wage of sin is death.

The commands of God cannot be evaluated by a computer. The wisdom of man is still as foolishness to Him. Dare we defy or even ignore our Maker?

A Lesson From Russia

THE ASSOCIATED PRESS recently reported a survey on religion made in one of the large Russian cities — Kazan, with a population of 900,000.

This city is 200 miles from Moscow. Two years were required to make the study.

The survey was the first of its kind in fifty years in an area where every effort was made on the part of the Soviets to destroy religious faith.

Results of the survey were published in the official magazine of Soviet atheism, *Nauka i Religiya*. The magazine did not say why it published the results of the survey, but the Associated Press suggests that it was apparently done as a warning that religion still has a hold on a considerable portion of the population.

Four hundred students at the city's university and representatives of its medical institute were used to make the study which included a house-to-house canvass of thousands of homes.

Despite the hazards of revealing their faith, 21 per cent of those contacted admitted belief in some religion.

Only 3 per cent who admitted to a religious faith were under 30 years of age, stark evidence of the effect of the anti-religious campaign conducted by the government, particularly among the youth in school.

Among some of the more interesting points developed in the survey were:

34 per cent of the believers belong to the working class.

42 per cent were men and women on old age pensions.

17 per cent were housewives.

The report indicated that "the educational level of believers is not high." This is in marked contrast to a recent Gallup survey of the same kind conducted in the United States. The Gallup survey showed that 45 per cent of all Americans go to church every week, and of them, the best educated are the best church goers.

In the United States, 48 per cent of the college students attended church; 44 per cent in high school attended, and 43 per cent of those in elementary schools went to church regularly.

One of the most important points brought out in the Russian survey was this, as quoted by the Associated Press:

"Having religious parents was described as the main reason for belief in religion among those surveyed. This was said to have been true in 80 per cent of the cases."

This is the great lesson to be gleaned from the Russian survey.

Let us keep in mind that the government there carried on a relentless campaign against religion. And let us keep in mind too that there are hazards in belonging to a church of any kind in Russia.

Yet in spite of these hazards and the impact of the anti-God drive of the Soviets, in 80 per cent of the cases where religious faith survived, it was among people whose parents had taught them, as children, to believe in God.

Then can anyone doubt the value of religious training in the home? Should any Latter-day Saint hesitate to hold regular family evenings, to have daily family prayer, to live the Gospel principles as a part of our daily lives?

No one can discount the value of such training. And everyone should have it.

Families which fail to hold family evenings regularly, as advised by the Presiding Brethren, deprive themselves of one of their greatest assets in good family living.

Families which fail to teach the Gospel to their children as a part of their daily routine, who fail to pray, to live the moral code and the Word of Wisdom, to honor the Sabbath Day, to uphold their Church leaders, to pay their financial obligations and otherwise establish a true Christian atmosphere in their homes, handicap themselves most seriously.

Those who rear their families in the faith will have joy both here and hereafter in the stalwart faith and high character of their loved ones.

The Peacemakers

MOST PEOPLE MIGHT well ask themselves how "Christian" they are.

The majority of Americans profess Christian belief, although actual church membership includes but a slight majority of the population. Yet most people in our country, even though they are not actively enrolled in any denomination, would say they believe in God and accept Christ as their Savior.

But what does it mean to accept Him as our Savior? Can it mean anything less than accepting His way of life and endeavoring to follow His pattern of living? Is this what it means to be Christian?

If this is so, just how "Christian" are we?

Our nation is rocked by stress of many kinds. In many cities large areas have been burned and pillaged by rioters, most of whom admit to a Christian belief.

Crime is increasing rapidly. Yet most criminals confess — even on death row — that they have a Christian belief, or at least what they think is a Christian belief.

Robberies, defalcations, immorality, killings, assaults are reaching frightening proportions, most of which are perpetrated by people who, deep in their hearts, admit to a form of Christian belief.

Even shoplifters, who are mostly women and children, attend Sunday School and other religious meetings. They profess to be Christians. But are they?

Are traffic offenders, who deliberately break the law if no officer is near, practicing their Christian religion as they do so? Most of them are supposed to be Christians.

In the depths of the despair which has come to so many as a result of the near-civil war which has swept some of our cities, and in recognition of the mounting rate of other criminality and sin, many are persuaded to ask themselves:

"Are we really a Christian nation?"

The Savior taught that we are known by our fruits, and that a good tree will not produce bad fruit, neither will a bad tree bring forth good fruit.

If our fruits are bad, can we claim to be real Christians?

The good "tree" of Christianity will never bring forth bad fruit. It cannot, for true Christianity comes from God; and God is GOOD. But if we as Christians bring forth bad fruit, then let us ask how really Christian we are.

Christianity teaches us to love our neighbors as ourselves. Is this practiced among our rioters and other destructive citizens?

Christianity teaches us the Golden Rule, saying: "All things whatsoever ye would that men should do to you, do ye even so to them." Does that describe the intent of the enemy of law and order?

Christianity tells the worshipper that if he has aught against his brother, or vice versa, he should go to that individual, work out a reconciliation, and then offer his gift at the altar of God. How much of this doctrine rests deep in the heart of the average person?

Christianity says: "Judge not, that ye be not judged." How far removed are the actions of those who defame the names of good men for political purposes, for example, or of those who jump to conclusions based on unfair publications or whispering campaigns!

Christianity says: "Thou shalt not commit adultery," and yet the nation's immorality rate is shocking, and with it the incidence of the frightful diseases that arise only from that condition.

Christianity says: "Thou shalt not lie, thou shalt not steal, thou shalt not kill." It tells us that we should sustain government in establishing law and order, and it teaches mercy, kindness, forgiveness, patience and long-suffering.

It condemns duplicity, misrepresentation and devious methods. It rebukes hypocrisy in the sharpest terms.

But it blesses those who feed the poor, clothe the naked, visit the sick, the needy and those in prison. It honors honesty, purity, and simplicity. It opposes worldliness, but exalts righteousness.

In America we have millions of good people, devout Christians, God-fearing men and women who are indeed good neighbors, upright citizens, provident, merciful and kind.

They are the backbone of America. They do not make the headlines. They do not cause the riots nor the upsurge of criminality, nor are they afflicted with the diseases of filthiness.

They are the good citizens, the ones who practice Christian virtues. How thankful we should be for them! They make America great.

But those who bring shame upon our country, and yet profess belief in Christ's name, may well remember that unless we do the works of Christ, we can hardly profess to follow Him.

It is righteousness which exalteth a nation.

True Safety Only In Faith

IN THESE TROUBLED times, why do people turn away from God? Why do they reject the only power which can "make and preserve us a nation"?

Our nation was founded by God-fearing men, and it prospered under their influence. It can only continue to prosper by following the same pattern.

"New morality" and "new freedom" and "new security" can never save us. They will only demoralize us.

The "new morality" is no morality at all. It is virtual free love. Can it preserve our nation?

"New freedom" is disrespect for law, and for the rights of others. It is a type of individualism that is destructive of "freedom under law," which is the only kind of liberty that can live. When "new freedom" is found to be lawlessness, it is recognized for what it really is — anarchy.

So-called "new security" is equally dangerous, but in a different way. It places the load of responsibility always upon "the other fellow." It destroys individual initiative, and teaches the false premise that "the world owes me a living."

All three of these "new" ideologies are contrary to the principles of our founding fathers, and all three are opposed to the basic doctrines of Christ. God-fearing men would never subscribe to any of them. That is why our founding fathers, who relied upon the Almighty, refused to countenance them.

As Latter-day Saints in America we are both citizens of the kingdom of God and of the nation which He founded.

God raised up America, with a definite purpose in mind. And He raised up the founding fathers to write an inspired document which has served us well as our national Constitution. He has seen us through war after war when our liberties have been challenged. He literally both "made and preserved us a nation."

Many of our great leaders of the past have told us that our nation will never be conquered from without, but they have warned that it might easily disintegrate from within. They have said further that such disintegration would begin, if ever it should come, with our failure to recognize the Almighty as our Founder, and to serve Him and uphold His precepts.

Their warnings have been disregarded in many respects.

One-third of our population is not enrolled in any church. Yet it must be said to our credit that many not enrolled formally in denominations do attend services on Sundays to swell the total figure of church attendance in this land to 45 per cent.

Of the 55 per cent who do not attend, many live in violation of divine laws which have been handed down to us. But they are not alone. Some of the so-called pious are insincere. Many of them are ignorant of the true meaning of faith, and as a result fail to live up to His precepts.

The "new morality" is invading Christian ranks, even being advocated by some clergymen. But it is nothing less than adulterous, and is completely contrary to the teachings of Christ.

If America is to save itself, this is one of the points on which she must act, and now. America cannot survive in immorality. It must return to the chastity taught in the scriptures.

And neither can America survive in the "new freedom" which would promote anarchy and a breakdown of law and order. There can be no immunity from the law for anyone. Political expediency cannot justify it. Constitutional law was established "for the rights and protection of all flesh, according to just and holy principles," the Lord declared.

When that divine principle is violated, we strike at the heart of the nation.

Another divine law says that we must earn our bread by the sweat of our face. There is no substitute for the law of work. When anyone endeavors to set up a system by which he or the masses may survive without effort, he builds upon the shifting sands, and his house will fall. No "united order" will succeed unless it is operated under the true inspiration of heaven. God's purposes are not to provide security only. They are to develop progress founded upon individual initiative which alone can bring the soul growth God requires of us.

The Almighty teaches productivity, work, effort, self-reliance, and says that if we fail to "bring forth much fruit" we shall lose our talents.

Our national survival can rest only upon faith in and obedience to God.

Manmade philosophies which break down morals, promote lawlessness, and plant the seeds of irresponsibility can only destroy.

A return to the Almighty and His divine principles is our only salvation.

The Sum Of The Whole Matter

In THIS DAY of pressure groups, lobbies, vested interests and over-selling of one ideology as against another, many people are left in a state of confusion.

The question of what to believe and which way to go becomes ever more important in their minds.

President David O. McKay, in his prophetic role, gave us a key to follow which is the path to safety. Said he:

"In these days of uncertainty and unrest, liberty-loving people's greatest responsibility and paramount duty is to preserve and proclaim the freedom of the individual, his relationship to Deity, and the necessity of obedience to the principles of the Gospel of Jesus Christ. Only thus will mankind find peace and happiness."

It is remembered that the Book of Mormon mentions difficult times in which every effort was made to find peace. Then it is recorded that only through the preaching of the word of God did peace come, for the preaching of the word was more powerful even than the sword.

Elder Harold B. Lee gave us a summation of this great principle also when he said at a recent conference:

"The conclusions we must reach are inescapable as we ponder these profound declarations —

"One who has an abiding conviction concerning God:

"Who has faith in his relationship to Deity:

"And the necessity of obedience to the Gospel of Jesus Christ:

"Who believes in and has a love for the Son of God, and

"Who has a feeling of certainty as to the immortality of the soul:

"Can successfully combat sin and unrighteousness IN ANY GUISE."

These principles sum up the entire matter of present-day conflicts and dangers.

If we would live the Gospel fully, we would be so fortified by it that we could and would resist sin and deceit, no matter in what guise they might appear.

We then would not be tempted by the worldly fashions of the day, because God has taught us modesty.

We would not be persuaded by alluring advertising of liquor and tobacco, because God has given us the Word of Wisdom.

We would not covet, for God has forbidden it.

We would not be weakened by the so-called "new morality" which is no morality at all, because God has taught us the law of chastity.

We would not be persuaded to join any rioting or other unlawful movement, because an article of our faith teaches us to honor and sustain the law.

We would not be lured into Communistic circles, because Communism is anti-Christ, and therefore opposed to all that the Lord teaches us.

We would not steal, nor lie, deceive, nor misrepresent, neither in business nor in gossip nor in any of our relationships with our fellowmen, because — "We believe in being honest, true, chaste, benevolent. . . ."

We would not take advantage of anyone for any reason, because we would live by the Golden Rule, doing to others as we would be done by.

We would not feel obliged to find expression for our talents in any oblique manner, because our allegiance to our Church affiliations would be complete, and we would give to them our time and our talents for the building of the kingdom of God.

We would never need to compromise our standards, expecting to gain advantage with people or organizations, because we would know that we cannot serve God and mammon at the same time.

So, as we study the Gospel, we may know that it provides a full and complete way of life, and that if we are "Gospel-centered" in our thinking and in our doing, all other things will fall into their logical places, easily brushed aside if we recognize them as being evil.

And thus fortified, as Elder Lee has said, the soul "can successfully combat sin and unrighteousness in any guise."

And as President McKay emphasized, "Only thus will mankind find peace and happiness."

Keep Home Fires Burning

In the first World War one of our favorite songs was the stimulating "Keep the Home Fires Burning."

That song carried a great message. Without the burning fires of home support, where would the boys receive encouragement as they fought a bitter enemy?

The strength of home ties added power to their arms, zest to their spirits and warmth to their hearts. Without these there would have been no victory.

Today we are in another conflict in which our boys fight and die for their country. Again the home fires must send out a glow which can reassure each fighting man that Dad and Mother, wife and children, brothers and sisters, uphold the traditions of true Americanism for which he fights.

But how are we to keep those home fires burning?

Is it done through pleasure seeking? Through moral breakdown? Through greed for more business and more profits? Through political chicanery?

What makes the home fires bright and attractive and good?

To have home fires, we must first have a home. Where is the "home fire" without a home, a good home?

Do our homes "pass muster," to use a military expression? What makes a home good?

President McKay gave us this definition: "A true home is one in which, if Christ should chance to enter, He would be pleased to linger and to rest."

In further definition he added: "Let us be more determined to make beautiful homes, to be kinder husbands, more thoughtful wives, more exemplary parents to our children, determined that in our homes we are going to have just a little taste of heaven here on this earth."

The strength of the nation depends upon the home. If the home fires are not bright and good, the nation languishes, and our fighting men on the front will languish too.

Good homes must rest upon a serious effort to live the Gospel of Christ. The Gospel provides every inducement to have good homes, and it gives the formula by which they may be good.

God is love. The home must be one of holy and sanctified love. God must be there, through the power of love.

Each member of the family must love the other as himself. Each must do to the other as he would be done by. Each must recognize the rights of the other, and abide by them.

Each must know that there can be no true love in wickedness. Each must learn too that when one sins, all are hurt, and no one has the right to hurt another.

The enemies of a good home are many.

Selfishness is the first. Out of selfishness come quarrels, misunderstandings, and often divorce. It promotes evil habits too. Is there a drinker, for example, who is not selfish in his attempt to gratify an unrighteous appetite? And is there a drinker who brings anything but unhappiness and even heartbreak upon a home? Does liquor weaken or strengthen family ties? "Fire water," as it is called, can hardly brighten the home fires or make them good.

Selfishness brings debt, and debt has broken up many a household. Can it brighten the home fires and strengthen the family?

Selfishness invites immorality too. Who submits to immorality except for selfish purposes and gratification?

Was there ever a crime which did not originate in selfishness? Was a character ever strengthened by it?

If selfishness is a prevailing factor in a home, can it be a great home? Can it keep burning the kind of fires which warm the heart, build family ties, strengthen a community and sustain a boy in a foxhole?

Obedience in the home is basic to obeying the law of the land. If the home is without order and righteous discipline, can we expect those who live there to respect the constitutional requirements of our government? Do riots keep the home fires burning? Does violence? Do self-opinionated groups which demand their "rights" regardless of the cost to others? Can communities or nations live in lawlessness and survive?

When all is said, good homes are founded upon faith in God whose Gospel teaches all the elements of good living and proper relationships. Only through the Gospel may we find true righteousness, and only righteousness "exalteth a nation."

To keep the home fires burning, we must keep alive our faith in Christ, and brighten the spark of divinity which is in each one of us.

Day Of Mourning

THREE ASSASSINATIONS OF national significance have shocked America and the world.

Following each of them, national days of mourning have been declared by the president of the United States. Flags were lowered to half-staff, special church services were held by most denominations, thousands wept as they passed by the biers of the fallen men, and the conditions which gave rise to such assassinations were soundly condemned.

But little if anything was done to correct the conditions of which these grievous crimes were but symptoms.

Mourning is indeed appropriate at times like these, both national and individual. But more than for the men who were ruthlessly cut down we should mourn over the conditions which gave rise to these outrages.

Our mourning should be so deep that it will force action of a significant nature. It is good to pass new laws to curb the unlawful use of guns, to place armed guards about political candidates and their families, and to make speeches of sympathy.

But guns, guards and speeches will not bring America back to its senses and to the equilibrium of law-abiding living which should characterize this great land.

America, like Europe, is suffering from a tragic deterioration of both individual and national character.

It seems that in both areas, right is sacrificed for what seems to be expedient. Pleasure has become more important than goodness. Security is sacrificed for ease of living. It is no longer esteemed smart to be honest, and virtue is looked upon as both old-fashioned and prudish.

The foundation of all good character is being abandoned in wholesale measure, which foundation is true religion, without which there can be no good character. And neither will stability and good character ever return without it.

What is the already obvious result of this ebbing of the tide of faith?

Immorality is increasing at a frightening rate, even on high school and college campuses. Crime rates are soaring. True family life is being abandoned. Millions of people now refuse to work, preferring to live lives of ease and corruption on public doles.

We coddle criminals and make law enforcement both difficult and unpopular. We foster extended use of alcoholic beverages.

In movies and TV we glamorize unchastity, crime and violence, giving our youth a form of education which can only reap the whirlwind.

What is the answer? More laws? More budget appropriations? More political speeches, more liberalizing of our statutes?

Neither money, speeches nor congressional acts will solve this problem. Only one thing will.

But will America accept it? There was a similar crisis in the past, and then the populace accepted the remedy. Will we be as wise as they were?

In the days of our Civil War, Lincoln knew the answer and clearly pointed it out.

"We have forgotten God," he declared to the nation. "We have grown in numbers, wealth and power as no other nation has ever grown, but we have forgotten the Gracious Hand which preserved us in peace and multiplied and enriched and strengthened us. We have vainly imagined in the deceitfulness of our hearts that all these blessings were produced by success. We have become too self-sufficient to feel the need of redeeming grace, too proud to pray to that God who made us."

Lincoln's indictment of conditions in his own time is startlingly applicable to our own.

How appropriate are the further words of his proclamation:

"It behooves us then, to humble ourselves before the offended Power, to confess our national sins, and pray for clemency and forgiveness."

Only a return to God can save America. But it must be sincere and genuine. It will require deep repentance on the part of all, and an unswerving obedience to His divine laws.

The Value Of Discipline

THE NATIONAL ASSOCIATION of Radio Broadcasters recently gave an award to Station WINA in Charlottesville, Virginia, for its editorial on the subject of discipline.

Among other things, this editorial said:

"Discipline is the very basis of civilization. Without a system of rules to live by and without law and order imposed by some group upon another, there would be no civilization.

"The root meaning of a word more nearly explains the whole context of ideas with which it is legitimately associated than the public's mistaken use of the same word.

"Coming from the Latin, 'to discipline' means 'to teach.' Discipline makes specific requirements of the individual; there is a system of punishments associated with discipline, and always the main objective is to preserve the interests and further the opportunity of the cooperative majority.

"This last is one part of discipline that many do not and will not recognize: that there is a counterpart to discipline — the ability to learn and to accept responsibility in a mature manner.

"Discipline produces these characteristics in a person when administered properly.

"Then why has there been such a fear of discipline — parents being concerned about disciplining their children — many young people rebelling against discipline as a threat to their freedom — mankind in general looking at discipline with a wary eye as a possible threat to liberty?

"Every normal person needs to have some sort of contest, some feelings of resistance, before he can make the best of his faculties.

"Whatever experience serves to give him the confidence that he can compete with other men helps to increase his solidarity with other men.

"The pendulum is swinging back to more discipline in each individual life. There is beginning to be an understanding that a good loving parent demands discipline. A good teacher demands discipline.

"And most important, the child or the student RESPECTS THE GOOD DISCIPLINARIAN a great deal more than the parent or teacher who does not demand anything of him."

Radio Station KDAL in Salina, Kansas, referred to the subject this way:

"Youngsters need to know they will be held responsible for their actions. They need to know they will never be able to escape from police records. Young people and adults should have this reminder before them, which was issued by an Illinois judge before sentencing two juveniles:

" 'You young men have been convicted of a felony. I am not sending you to prison, but you should know the record of your conviction will stand as long as this courthouse stands.

" 'If you are called as a witness in any court you will be asked if you have ever been convicted of a felony. You will have to answer yes. You may need a surety bond to cover a position of trust. Your record means you probably will be refused by most bonding companies. In a few years you will be 21. Others your age will be allowed to vote. You will be denied this privilege. I am granting you a parole. A parole is in no sense a pardon. Your conviction is now a matter of record. It will be with you to the end of your days.' "

Radio Station KSL commented in this way:

"Facts are facts. The next time the choice is yours whether or not to engage in some questionable activity, remember you are not just choosing for today. It's your entire future you are shaping."

It is good to hear such comments from important radio station commentators. It is good to know that the pendulum is swinging back to common sense in regard to discipline, punishment and youth development.

The Lord cannot be wrong. The Bible quotes Him repeatedly in favor of proper discipline. It teaches clearly that there are rules laid down for righteousness, and that to the breaking of each law a punishment is affixed. Wrongdoers will reap the results of their acts. We will be held accountable on judgment day for every deed committed in the flesh.

Each act makes a mark on our character. It also shapes our reputation.

Persons who say that it is wrong to discipline a child simply do not know the facts of life.

Parents who have been misled by this widespread but mistaken philosophy would do well to look into the scripture for some inspired advice, part of which is: "Spare the rod and spoil the child."

A Covenant Nation

FOR YEARS THE United States Senate was inspired by the prayers and public utterances of its chaplain, Dr. Peter Marshall. He has been forgotten by many of the present generation, and some now in Congress never knew this great man.

Peter Marshall was a scholar of deep perception. He knew the meaning of true Americanism, and constantly pointed the way to the ultimate goal of this nation. He spoke of the American Dream and held it constantly before his listeners.

"It is a dream," he said, "that has shone brightly at times and that has faded at other times."

In the book *A Man Called Peter,* compiled by his wife Catherine, he still teaches his excellent philosophy:

"World events," he says, "are forcing us, whether we realize it or not, to rediscover the meaning and the significance of the things that make America different from other nations, the hope of a world weary of war, heartsick and hungry.

"What is the American Dream? What is it that makes our country different?

"What is America? Where is our country going?

"Let no answer be lightly made. We cannot speak with truth or realism about the future unless we understand the past.

"What has America to give to the rest of the world? If only grain or money or clothing or armaments, then we have already lost the war and the peace . . . and our own souls.

"Ours is a covenant nation, the only surviving nation on earth that had its origins in the determination of the Founding Fathers to establish a settlement to the glory of God and the advancement of the Christian faith.

"That was what William Bradford and George Carver had in mind when beneath the swinging lantern in the cabin of the "Mayflower," they affixed their signatures to the solemn declaration which established the Commonwealth of Massachusetts.

"They had come from the Old World and were seeking refuge in the new. They had come from tyranny and oppression, they had come from fear and coercion, they had come from famine and from difficulty, from wars and threats of wars. They sought a new life in a new land.

"Religious liberty to worship God according to the dictates of one's own conscience . . . and equal opportunity for all men . . . these were the twin pillars of the American Dream.

"Now a Covenant Nation is one that recognizes its dependence upon God and its responsibility toward God.

"This nation was so born. God was recognized as the source of human rights. The Declaration of Independence says so.

"A Covenant Nation is one which recognizes God. His purposes stand over and above the nation. The highest role the nation can play is to reflect God's righteousness in national policy.

"There have been periods in our history when the American Dream has faded and grown dim. Today there is real danger that the American Dream will become the Forgotten Dream.

"For freedom is not the right to do as one pleases, but the opportunity to please to do what is right.

"The Founding Fathers sought freedom.

". . . Not from the law but freedom in law;

"not freedom from government, but freedom in government;

"not freedom from speech, but freedom in speech;

"not freedom from the press, but freedom in the press;

"not freedom from religion, but freedom in religion.

"We need to ponder these things today," concluded the great Marshall.

Our Honored Dead

"GREATER LOVE HATH no man than this, that a man lay down his life for his friends."

So spoke the Savior as He is quoted in the fifteenth chapter of John. He uttered this great truth as He gave to His disciples one of His great injunctions:

"This is my commandment, That ye love one another, as I have loved you."

"And then He added: "Ye are my friends, if ye do whatsoever I command you."

The Savior well understood the giving of one's life for his friends. He knew that before long He himself would do that very thing, and not only for his friends but for all mankind, because His atonement affects us all.

There are many in the world who give their lives for their friends, and the most numerous are our servicemen who so bravely face death to preserve the rights and freedoms of our people.

Letters from servicemen are often published in the papers, particularly if those letters were written by some who had a foreboding of death.

Those boys who die in battle, as far as we know, do so willingly. Not that they want to die — quite the opposite. They want to live, to come back home, and to enjoy the blessings of peace and quiet and family life. They hope to go to school, and develop careers for the future.

But they face enemy fire, and die. In their supreme sacrifice they give up family and friends, careers and pleasures, and the only peace and quiet they obtain is found in a hero's grave.

Most of them die with a sense of resignation, which is a willingness to make the sacrifice, since to them it appears necessary and important.

And in giving their lives, they show their love for us, for their families, and for their flag.

We cannot blame God for war. We bring wars upon ourselves. Most of us hate war. But as citizens who follow our leaders, we are duty bound under the Constitution to respond to the call to arms when that call comes. For that reason, Latter-day Saints, as loyal citizens, defend their flag.

The Lord by revelation justifies His people in defending our Constitution, and if that defense requires the blood of some of our people, so be it. We of today or most of us, we hope, feel like Patrick Henry expressed himself: "Give me liberty or give me death."

Liberty is free agency, as we express it in our Church vocabulary, and free agency is God-given. It is vital to our progress. It is divine.

Our men who march to war and give their lives in the honorable defense of their country fit into the definition of the Lord's words. They have that greater love. They give their lives for their friends.

Families who lose their boys may take comfort in this great fact. They may know too that the Lord is a God of love, and that true love will not go without its reward.

We do not know all of God's plans. We are but finite souls, and much of the time we "see through a glass darkly," as Paul expressed it.

But God is infinite, as is also His love. So are His mercy and His grace.

As the author of love, will He not remember with compassion those who loved their friends and their country so well that they gave their lives to defend them?

Will there not be a martyr's reward for such as they? Will they not be given some added consideration when on Judgment Day He evaluates their lives and their deeds? Will there not be some special understanding, some extraordinary sympathy between Him, who made the supreme sacrifice on the cross, and those who made their ultimate sacrifice on the battlefield?

And should there not be hope in all our hearts that the sacrifices of war may be brought to an end by a repentant world willing to accept the true meaning of that sacrifice on Calvary?

He knew love. And He knew sacrifice. He is the Prince of Peace, and will give us peace if we will but follow Him.

Where Is Good Character?

WHEN WE LATTER-DAY Saints refer to our Article of Faith which includes the statement, "We believe in being true," we must keep in mind a proper definition of loyalty.

With it also we must remember the vital necessity of standing by principle, refusing to vacillate with every wind of circumstance.

It is well for us to remember the examples of our Pioneer forefathers who laid their all upon the altar of God. Their religion meant so much to them that they left their homes, moved from place to place seeking freedom of religion, and even died for it as many did on the plains, at Haun's Mill, at Carthage or elsewhere as they were required to make a stand. Shall we do less?

We today are witnessing in the world a most tragic development. It is a wholesale breakdown of good character. It is seen in our highest and most respected bodies. Not even Congress is exempt. It is seen in the rioting of students, racist groups and others, mostly fanned by Communist agitators.

The refusal of many to assume responsibility is a frightening aspect of it. Thousands now refuse to work or support their families. Doles are preferable for them. Fraud is seen even in charities, one of the worst examples being women who actually go into the "business" of having illegitimate children as a means of increasing their government allotments.

The resurgence of crime, of course, is another evidence of the condition. Some community leaders ignore the need for better law enforcement. Individual citizens often refuse to come to the aid of persons attacked by desperadoes. Able-bodied boys sit idly by as their girl companions are seized and carried off by hoodlums to a fate worse then death.

Politics become more and more corrupt. Public servants under oath, "bite the hand that feeds them." Perjury is no longer shunned by some in the courts. Certain judges render decisions favoring criminals and hurting the public whom they are pledged to serve and protect.

Some clergymen have endorsed free love in the guise of the "new morality" which is no morality at all. Likewise have some educators and political leaders.

Demonstrators have waved Communist flags in our streets while denouncing the government. Our flag has been burned. If there is public resentment at these acts of treason, it is kept eloquently quiet.

What has become of our good character? Where is loyalty? Where is principle?

It is part of the religion of every Latter-day Saint to be "true" as the Articles of Faith say, true, honest and virtuous.

We must be true to every high principle, to good character, to the advancement of righteousness. We must be true to our loved ones and not besmirch their good names by our wrongful acts. We must be true to our flag and to our boys who fight and die in Vietnam.

Those who hold public trust must be true to the highest traditions of honesty and integrity. It is part of our religion so to do.

Those who teach must build character, never weaken it. Otherwise they are not true.

Employers must be true to their workers and make Christian ideals a part of their personal relations programs. Employees must be true to their employers, giving them honest production. They must be true to their families whose living they earn, and true to the Church in which they hold membership, never bringing any reflection upon it because of poor performance.

Boys and girls must likewise be true. They must learn the value of high principle and come to know that to vary from it can bring only disaster. They must be loyal to their parents, never feeling that father and mother are their enemies merely because of an occasional act of discipline.

Proper discipline is a part of our education, and is incident to the growing-up process. All must learn which way is right. All must learn to avoid pitfalls, and when we make mistakes we must be willing to make the necessary adjustments.

Parents are not our enemies because they chastise us. What they do in righteousness is in our own interest.

Parents, of course, must be true also, and honest with their children. They must ever be fair in their judgments and righteous in their discipline. This, too, is part of good character.

As individuals and as nations, we can never survive without good character. To suppose that we can sin with impunity or get gain by rebelling against just principles, is simply an unsound and dangerous presumption.

And what gives us our true sense of righteous values? It is the Gospel of Christ. It is His Church.

To keep our balance, let us keep close to the Church and accept the direction of the inspired men whom God has chosen to lead us.

The Rights Of Non-Criminals

EVERY PERSON HAS the right to life, liberty and the pursuit of happiness.

This includes the victims of criminals, as well as the criminals. It includes an assurance that our courts will be as fair to law-abiding citizens as they are to those who break the law. It provides that if any preferred treatment is to be given, it should favor the good citizens rather than the parasites on society.

This was the substance of the thinking of a group of women in Indianapolis who started an anti-crime crusade in that city which now has reached the proportions of a major movement.

Fifty thousand women there have now organized to fight crime, and part of their objective is to see that judges in the courts deal fairly with the victims of crime.

It started five years ago following the death of a 90-year-old woman killed by a 15-year-old boy who snatched her purse. But there had been numerous previous crimes of a similar nature. Especially purse-grabbings and sex assaults on women walking alone on the streets of the city.

A significant drop in crime has been the result.

The President's Crime Commission, referring to this movement, said:

"The most dramatic example in the country of a citizens' group that has addressed itself forcefully and successfully to the problems of crime and criminal justice is the Anti-Crime Crusade of Indianapolis."

These women give complete support to their local police, who in turn cooperate with the women. Their program includes:

Putting proper lighting on city streets.

Getting school drop-outs back into school.

Providing jobs for boys who need them.

Assisting boys released from penal institutions to adjust properly in society.

And setting up a system of "court watching."

The latter point was considered by the women as one of their most important tasks. At least two of their number sat in on every court case, and reported back to the entire group on the practices and decisions of the courts.

They decided that it is the right of the public to demand efficient, mannerly operation of the courts. And this they achieved.

But education in law observance was also given. With the cooperation of school and police officials, all students in the seventh and eighth grades were provided with special instruction on maintaining the law and the advantages of doing so.

More than 2,000 drop-outs were put back in school without spending tax funds. The streets are now well lighted. Women and girls may walk safely at night. Even the debris around the city has been removed.

But it is brought more and more to the attention of the public that keeping youth in line is first a matter of keeping adults in line.

Statistics of the past several years have shown a sharp increase in the number of young people arrested for serious crimes — murder, robbery, forcible rape, burglary, aggravated assault, larceny of $50 or more and automobile theft.

Those under 18 years of age account for almost half the total arrests reported for these crimes.

In a concentrated effort to control this rash of youthful criminality, innumerable youth-serving groups have joined law enforcement movements.

These groups, often desperately in need of support, offer the community a good opportunity to combat crime, since youthful criminality is uniquely suited to prevention and correction.

However, these efforts in behalf of youth can only supplement — never replace — parental concern.

Broken homes, dissolute parents and a tragic absence of guidance typify the backgrounds of many youthful offenders.

The role of the parent is paramount. It is indeed difficult to imagine a more fundamental service to society than imbuing one's children with respect for law and order.

The Home Is The Answer

A STABILIZED HOME, in which religious instruction forms a major part, is the only real answer to juvenile delinquency.

This is the consensus of opinion of scholars who have made a serious study of the causes and prevention of delinquency.

These scholars say that parents and children alike must be taught how to live together as a family: their home must be "God-centered," and must be associated with a church which provides an uplifting, character-building program for the youth.

They list two kinds of homes: one which produces delinquency, and the other which seldom has youth problems.

The poor home in which delinquency thrives is described as one in which there is no genuine love between father and mother, nor between parents and children; no regular family routine in the home, no preparation, no planning; no fixed time for meals, no set time to come in at night, nor to do homework, nor to go to bed; no discipline nor rules of conduct; no group activity and little or no religion and moral training.

Such a home usually has in it parents who drink and who give their own children liquor at home; parents who quarrel, even in the presence of their children;

who party and carouse, who are often untruthful, dishonest, careless about paying bills, give their children no training in financial matters, provide no companionship for children and have no respect for religious matters.

J. Edgar Hoover, our great head of the FBI, explained that juvenile delinquents seldom if ever come from homes in which:

"1 — Parents try to understand their children and find time to cultivate their friendship and love.

"2 — Parents of integrity face facts and live by the truth.

"3 — Parents live within their means and give their children examples in thrift, security and stability.

"4 — Parents are industrious and teach their children that most of life's good things come only from hard work.

"5 — Parents have worthwhile goals in life and seek to have their children join them in their attainment.

"6 —Parents have common sense, a capacity for friendship and a sense of humor.

"7 — Parents live in harmony with each other and do not quarrel in the presence of their children.

"8 — Parents have ideals and a compelling urge to serve rather than to be served.

"9 — Parents are unswervingly loyal to their own children, but can express righteous indignation and chastise them when necessary. (That old proverb 'Spare the rod and spoil the child' is as valid today as it ever was.

"10 — Parents' decisions are controlled, not by what their children desire, but by what they need."

There is no doubt in the minds of scholars that for the most part delinquency or freedom from it is a result of home environment. The experts say that children are not born criminals, nor pampered parasites. They are made that way by the environment in which they live.

And children are not born as young ladies and gentlemen, honest, upright and clean, but are so as a result of their training.

This kind of philosophy makes more persuasive than ever the decree of the Lord in the 68th Section of the Doctrine & Covenants:

"And again, inasmuch as parents have children in Zion, or in any of her stakes which are organized, that teach them not to understand the doctrine of repentance, faith in Christ the Son of the living God, and of baptism and the gift of the Holy Ghost by the laying on of the hands, when eight years old, the sin be upon the heads of the parents.

"For this shall be a law unto the inhabitants of Zion, or in any of her stakes which are organized.

"And their children shall be baptized for the remission of their sins when eight years old, and receive the laying on of the hands.

"And they shall also teach their children to pray, and to walk uprightly before the Lord."

Christianity's Virility

THE UNFORTUNATE AND misconceived "God is dead" controversy is itself now dead, to all intents and purposes. It came to its deserved and sudden end about as quickly as it had arisen. For this all thinking people will be grateful.

But a wider question is now raised, actually related to the first, and in fact responsible for it. That question pertains to the virility of what the world knows as Christianity today. It is not dead, but is it dying?

A few weeks ago *Time* magazine reported the visit of the Pope to South America, and incidental thereto, quoted figures on the low church attendance in the great southern continent. They were appalling.

When less than 10 per cent of the population of an entire continent makes any pretense of practicing their religion, one immediately wonders about the virility of their faith, regardless of denomination.

But South America is not alone in this. Europe is very similar. About the same percentage of western Europeans go to church as is true of our southern continent. In Great Britain, the average ranges nearer 15 per cent, but even that leaves 85 per cent of the entire population not attending religious services.

With shocking figures like these before us, is it not time to ask if Christianity as the world now knows it is a dying religion?

It should be remembered too, that many people go to church out of no deep inward conviction and practice their rituals without ever being "born again," as the Savior expressed it.

Of course there are many believers — devoutly so in thousands of cases — who, like Abraham Lincoln, do not attend church services because they cannot accept the creeds which are presented there.

No one knows how many people truly believe in Christ. No census has ever explored this field. With many believers who attend no church, and with many who go to church for only superficial reasons, and with the vast majority not attending religious services at all, with or without faith, no one knows how many true believers there really are.

This is so not only in other lands but also in the United States. However, in this country, a Gallup poll does show 45 per cent of the people attending some religious meeting every week, which is most reassuring.

But how effective is the Christianity which most people know? It has not yet made them love their neighbors as themselves, it has not yet taught the masses to turn the other cheek, to forgive seventy times seven times, to love their enemies, or to live the Golden Rule. It has not yet taught all men to be honest, chaste, and truthful, or to live the Ten Commandments.

And if the kind of Christianity now known to mankind has not yet accomplished these basics, how effective is it?

The churches are in the worst turmoil they have ever known, at least since the Reformation. Even clergymen are denying their faith, leading others into agnos-

ticism. Many in the ministry — both men and women — are deserting their posts, not by tens, but by
hundreds and thousands.

Peter and Paul died for their faith, as did those
thrown to the lions in the Roman arenas. Who has
equal devotion today? Is it a different faith, that it no
longer moves people deeply?

Divisions, conflicts and internal strife mark most
large denominations today. Leaders are being repudi-
ated. Secularism is more potent than faith.

It all points up one thing: that the "faith that was
once delivered to the saints," as Jude expressed it,
is not the faith which today is embraced by many, and
which fails to hold adherents as did the ancient faith.

But God is wise. God is merciful. He knows that
nearly 2,000 years without revelation could lead to no
other condition. He would have given guidance if men
had sought it, but revelation and prophecy were rejected, and the world drifted into dark ages which, re-
ligiously speaking, still persist.

Yet in His mercy, the Almighty has given mankind
a new revelation of Himself, and has instituted a modern ministry to bring His true light into the world.

It is the Restored Gospel given through the Prophet
Joseph Smith. Heavenly light is again on earth; true
prophets minister again in the flesh and God speaks
once more to men. This light, and it alone, can bring
peace to our troubled world.

America's New Approach

THE INAUGURAL CEREMONIES of President Nixon sounded a distinctly spiritual tone.

Five prayers were offered by leading clergymen representing as many faiths. The Salt Lake Mormon Tabernacle Choir sang as though inspired. The Marine Band played "God Bless America," and the President's address pointed to a new horizon of spirituality.

It was all both satisfying and pleasing to thoughtful citizens. But the impressive prayer of the Reverend Billy Graham struck a note which deserves special consideration. He pointed to our need of national repentance as a prerequisite to obtaining divine help.

He was right. There can be no true spirituality without compliance with the laws of heaven. This all Americans must learn and accept.

It is frighteningly true that the blessings of God are predicated upon obedience to His law, and without that obedience, there can be no bestowal of His favor.

It is not enough merely to pray to the Lord, or to mention Him in our speeches, because neither prayer alone nor lip service will save anyone. The Lord is a God of works as well as of faith. Mere appeals for divine aid, urgent though they may seem to be, will not bring the desired results. Righteous works must accompany them.

It was once said that this nation cannot survive if it is "half slave and half free." But we can no more be halfway in our spirituality than we can be halfway about our freedom.

In Lincoln's day that great leader called his people to repentance and told them that they had forgotten God in the midst of their prosperity, that they had forgotten the gracious Hand that made them.

Such is nearly the case today. How many people now really put God first in their lives? How many Americans who listened in on the inaugural ceremonies are willing to set aside selfish interests to truly achieve peace on a basis of common brotherhood?

How many are willing to do unto others as they would be done by? How many will turn the other cheek or go the extra mile?

How many are strictly honest? How many soberly eschew liquor, drugs and other stimulants which destroy the ability to think clearly and which inflame tempers and cause tongues to babble meaninglessly?

How many in America are willing to observe the moral laws laid down by the God to whom they pray? Can prayers be meaningful and persuasive in heaven if they are uttered out of gluttony, dishonesty and lust?

Can a nation which pleads for divine help do so with any degree of effectiveness when it upholds a "new morality" which is no morality at all, and which opens the door to sex evils on a scale so wide that a plague of social disease descends upon us?

Billy Graham was right. If we are to expect divine aid in solving our problems, then as a nation we must turn quickly to the divine law and live it.

John the Baptist taught the wicked of his day, as they asked for divine guidance, to repent and bring forth fruits to prove that repentance had actually taken place.

James, in his straightforward epistle, taught that the "wrath of man worketh not the righteousness of God," and added, "be ye doers of the word, and not hearers only, deceiving yourselves."

Can anyone misunderstand him when he says also, "Faith without works is dead"?

With a new president, America has an opportunity now to open a new era. It can be one of righteousness and success; it can be a passive period with little change from the status quo; or it can become a morass of distress and failure brought about by the wickedness of the people. Now is the time of decision.

The Almighty indeed has called this a land of promise, but He has said that we who live here can receive His beneficence only as we serve the God of the land, who is Jesus Christ.

He will protect us from our enemies abroad — if we serve Him.

He will defeat our enemies from within — if we serve Him.

He will inspire our President — if he and if we in our prayers are sustained by righteous works.

And He will bless and guide our lawmakers — if they will put His divine purpose first in their lives.

Then indeed can "God bless America" become a reality — because she will deserve it.

The Church -- The Rock

WHERE IS SECURITY in the world today?

Where is protection from evil?

Where is a guiding light that may be followed safely to a harbor of refuge in the storms now afflicting the world?

The dove of peace has left the earth. The destroying angel is now at work. He spares no individual, no family, no community or nation.

Satan seems intent upon a total destruction of righteousness before his own power is taken away.

It is sad indeed that so much of humanity seems willing to fall into his schemes. Millions not only yield to his deceptions but actually delight in his seductions.

With all of its technological advancements, the world is plunging into a night of spiritual chaos.

But through it all, a divine light shines from heaven. In spite of almost universal turmoil there comes a proffer of divine security against which the gates of hell cannot prevail.

This light — this beacon — this rock of stability — is the Gospel of Jesus Christ, restored to earth in our day.

The Lord knew what conditions would face his modern Church. He knew that Satanic powers would seek to destroy it. But the Almighty decreed nevertheless that it shall roll forth until it fills the whole earth, undaunted by world conditions, unscathed by the attacks of its enemies, never to be destroyed nor given to another people.

As he re-established his Church the Lord said: "It is the eleventh hour, and the last time that I shall call laborers into my vineyard."

As if to rebuke the unbelievers he declared further:

"This Church have I established." No one need misunderstand that plain statement. It was an act of God.

"This is my gospel." Equally clear are these words, spoken concerning the teachings of the Prophet Joseph Smith.

"Upon this rock will I build my Church." Only the Gospel of Christ could form the foundation of this work.

That Gospel is now re-issued to the world, the one and only divine plan, once lost amid the darkness of the ages, but now brought forth again in shining reality.

It will move forward steadily, never to be impeded, as it prepares for the glorious Second Coming of the Son of God.

Two great movements are now proceeding simultaneously, preliminary to that great day. One is the forward progress of the restored Church of Jesus Christ. The other is the outpouring of the tribulations predicted in scripture.

Neither will interfere with the other. Both will move on unrestricted. Each will accomplish its own purposes.

But the Gospel — the Rock of Christ, the restored Church, the "body" of Christ — in the end will be triumphant, and the Saints eventually will be received by the glorious Redeemer at His coming.

In the midst of all the tribulations, and we see many of them today, the Church will continue to stand as a redoubtable refuge for the righteous of every nation.

It offers the only true security on earth today, for the Lord has promised that He will protect His Saints in the midst of world upheavals.

The Church has become a guiding light to mankind, pointing the way through darkness, leading each faithful soul to a harbor of peace.

The conferences it holds periodically are significant. For the Saints they bring renewed faith, fresh assurance, and added stimulus in carrying on the work of the Lord.

For mankind generally they bear a message of life, hope, forgiveness, and rehabilitation.

To a world that is losing its faith in God, what great comfort a new revelation of the Deity could bring! That revelation has come.

To a world confused by hundreds of differing creeds, what reassurance a certain knowledge of the revealed truth could provide! That truth has now been restored.

To a world torn by hate and bitterness, what added hope a new and divine message of peace could supply! That message is now among us, brought to earth through a modern revelation of God.

At general conference, once more these truths are proclaimed. God has spoken again!

Washington And Franklin

GEORGE WASHINGTON IS usually spoken of as the "father" of our country. But he was more than that. With the help of Benjamin Franklin, he literally preserved it from an early demise.

These two great men stood at the crossroads of this new republic as it was struggling for existence, threatened as it was with destruction by its own hand. Americans never can fully measure the debt of gratitude we owe to them.

Both felt within themselves that America was a land of destiny. Both acknowledged that the Almighty very largely had been instrumental in its creation as a nation. And both bowed in dismay as their shortsighted colleagues almost destroyed the inspired concept of freedom which we know today.

Their associates did not know the true meaning of political liberty. They had never heard of a "government of the people, by the people and for the people." Some of their thinking was still colored by royalist opinions.

Washington had repeated frequently his conviction that it was the Almighty who gave victory to the colonists. Knowing that the Divine Hand had thus set America free, it was revolting to him to see attempts made to neutralize all that had been done. With Franklin he opposed such tendencies throughout the convention, and finally prevailed.

Franklin was always his close ally. Together they had planned for the way of life we know today, and as Franklin saw the convention go week after week in fruitless debate, at times in bitter controversy, he began to wonder what form of government would finally evolve.

At one time he appealed to the convention to pray for guidance and for an end to all the controversy, but strangely enough he was rebuffed. Still his appeal has gone down in history as one of the great moments of the convention. In part he said:

"The small progress we have made after four or five weeks of close attendance and continual reasonings with each other, our sentiments differing on almost every question — producing almost as many noes as ayes, is, methinks, a melancholy proof of the imperfection of human understanding. . . .

"In this situation of this Assembly, groping as it were in the dark to find political truth, and scarce able to distinguish it when presented to us, how has it happened, Sir, that we have not hitherto once thought of humbly appealing to the Father of lights to illuminate our understandings?"

He then spoke of the many answers to prayers during the war for independence, and continued:

"To that kind Providence we owe this happy opportunity of consulting in peace on the means of establishing our future national felicity. And have we now forgotten that powerful Friend?

"I have lived, Sir, a long time, and the longer I live the more convincing proofs I see of this truth: That God governs in the affairs of men. . . .

"I firmly believe this," he continued, "and I also believe that without his concurring aid we shall succeed in this political building no better than the builders of Babel. We shall be divided by our little partial local interests; our projects will be confounded, and we ourselves shall become a reproach and a byword down to future ages. And what is worse, mankind may hereafter from this unfortunate instance despair of establishing governments by human wisdom and leave it to chance and war and conquest.

"I therefore beg leave to move that henceforth prayers imploring the assistance of heaven and its blessings on our deliberations, be held in this assembly every morning before we proceed to business, and that one or more of the clergy of this city be requested to officiate in that service."

His resolution set off a new round of debate, and was finally voted down. One of the main reasons given was that the new nation was without funds and could not pay the clergymen for this service. There was general embarrassment, but the motion failed.

When the time came to sign the new Constitution, all waited to see what Washington and Franklin would do. As they took the lead, discarded all thoughts of sectionalism, and signed the document, then and only then did the others follow.

Franklin himself regarded the creation of the Constitution as nothing short of a miracle in view of the nature of the debates. He saw in it the hand of the Almighty, despite the refusal of many of his colleagues even to join him in prayer.

It is a fact — God did raise up strong men to write the Constitution despite the antagonism of many of their colleagues. And this is all the more reason why we who live today should preserve it with equal diligence.

Lincoln's Mother

LITTLE IS KNOWN of President Abraham Lincoln's mother. That she was an exceptionally good mother is fully accepted. That she reared a son who became one of the great men of all time is recognized in many nations around the world.

As to his greatness, it is of more than passing interest that David Lloyd George, premier of England in World War I, said of him:

"I doubt whether any statesman who ever lived sank so deeply into the hearts of the people of many lands as Abraham Lincoln did.

"I am not sure that you in America realize the extent to which he is also our possession and our pride.

"His courage, fortitude, patience, humanity, clemency, his trust in the people, his belief in democracy, and, may I add, some of the phrases in which he gave expression to those attributes, will stand out forever as beacons to guide troubled nations and their perplexed leaders.

"Resolute in war, he was moderate in victory. Misrepresented, misunderstood, underestimated, he was patient to the last. But the people believed in him, and they still believe in him.

"In life he was a great American. He is an American no longer. He is one of those giant figures, of whom there are few in history, who lose their nationality in death. They are no longer Greek, or Hebrew, or English or American. They belong to mankind.

"I wonder whether I will be forgiven for saying that George Washington was a great American, but Abraham Lincoln belongs to the common people of every land."

What made Lincoln great? What gave him his great sense of justice? From whence came his mercy and compassion? What made him a "man of God" as he has been called by many?

Lincoln himself used to say: "All that I am or hope to be I owe to my angel mother."

And what made her such an angelic mother?

As one writer expressed it, she possessed "a sense of reverence that lifted her above the dull and deadly routine of the commonplace."

When John Wesley Hill wrote those words, he touched the very heart of the reason for both Abraham Lincoln's greatness and that of his mother.

She was reverent. And because she was reverent her son was likewise reverent. And that reverence could be born only of a deep faith in the God to whom she paid that reverence.

And so it was that her little boy grew up from infancy with reverence for God as a daily example, and with sincere regard for the sacred word.

No matter how hard those frontier days were, no matter how difficult it was to make a true home in a log cabin, to help run the farm, and care for an unpredictable husband, she made whatever sacrifice was necessary to teach faith to her children.

That faith was taught from the Bible, which was the favorite book of the household. She even chose biblical names for her children — Abraham and Sarah. Mother and children alike read the scriptures — studied them — prayed over them — together.

And mother and children sat down before the fireplace in a family group and pondered over lessons from the holy word, absorbing and learning to love the divine rules of right and wrong, of justice, and of mercy. These traits were born and bred into those children. And they bore fruit.

So where did Lincoln learn his consideration for the common people? Not alone from having been one of them; not only from having grown up in adversity. In many men this breeds resentment.

But as Lincoln read of the Savior teaching the common people, feeding them, healing them, even raising a poor widow's only son from the dead, he was impressed and inspired.

Out of his great reverence for the Redeemer and his desire to be like Him, Lincoln learned to love the common people, to sympathize with them, to help and to save them.

This created within him a deep hatred of slavery and injustice of all kinds. It inspired his desire to preserve a government of the people, by the people and for the people. It made him just and true.

When his mother lay dying, she said to him: "I am going away from you, Abraham, and shall not return. I know that you will be a good boy; that you will be kind to Sarah and your father. I want you to live as I have taught you, and love your Heavenly Father, and keep His commandments."

And this is what he did.

Casualties Of War

EACH WEEK THE nation counts its war casualties. They are listed as killed, wounded and missing.

These reports are most sobering, and wring the hearts of loved ones who had so fervently hoped that such a loss would never come to them. Every right-thinking American sympathizes deeply with their bereavement and constantly prays that the horrors of war will soon come to an end.

But there are other casualties that are seldom mentioned, casualties which should stagger this nation and compel every man who enters the service to pause and consider their causes.

These casualties are not the flower of America, shot down in defense of our flag. These are innocent babies born as the offspring of adulterous relationships between our soldiers and the women of the Orient.

Medical men warn of the skyrocketing rise of venereal disease among our forces, and it is certainly something to fear. But what of the innocent children born from such relationships?

No one knows exactly how many of these children are now living in Vietnam. The figure may run well beyond the 50,000 mark. In Japan there are known to be more than 20,000 mixed bloods fathered by U.S. servicemen, both white and black. The number of those whose fathers are black is estimated at between 2,000 and 3,000.

Other thousands of GI-fathered illegitimates are in Thailand, Korea and Taiwan.

Nearly all have been abandoned by their fathers who sought a momentary "thrill," as they thought, by cohabiting with Oriental women, not thinking that their own flesh and blood — born of these illicit unions — would become abandoned orphans, shunned by nearly all who see them.

Ebony magazine recently wrote of those born from black American GI's, and told of their rejection and utter hopelessness.

The magazine said that these are the first to be abandoned and the last to be adopted, and that those born of Negro fathers are "thrice damned."

In Japan they are kept in orphanages until they are sixteen, but then they are "on their own."

They become social outcasts, not accepted by anyone. Few will employ them. Seldom will landlords give them housing.

Particularly Negro half-bloods fight a hopeless battle in a hostile world. Homeless and jobless, most of them choose between a life of drudgery and a career of crime.

In Vietnam these unfortunates roam the streets, unwanted, uncared for, begging for a living.

It is said that one in every ten American soldiers — white or black — fathers a child by an Asian woman.

This is nothing new in war areas. The same thing happened in France and Germany following the last two world wars. In India the English created the Eurasians. The French produced the French-Indo-Chinese, and the Dutch the Dutch-Indonesians.

Now Americans are producing what Pearl Buck calls Amerasians.

But they are abandoned! They are neglected! Many are scorned and persecuted because of their birth!

The purpose of this writing is not to solve the problem of caring for these unfortunates. Rather, it is to remind American servicemen of their obligations.

Which of them has the right to have illegitimate children?

Which has the right to take the virtue of an Asian or any other girl or lose his own?

Which American — at home or abroad — has the right to abandon his own flesh and blood and forget that his illegitimate child ever existed?

Can the God of heaven, who holds us all accountable for our sins, overlook this wickedness?

Can America expect the blessings of heaven upon our war efforts when we are so impregnated with sin that many of our men not only violate the laws of morality, but do violence likewise to every principle of family relationship which God has made known to us?

What good are national days of prayer if we do not support our prayers by good works? Will God strengthen the arms of fighting men who desecrate His most holy laws? Will He prosper a nation which apparently condones these illicit practices and does little more than provide prophylactics to men who indulge?

Are our fathers — even of Amerasians — so lacking in a natural affection that they are willing to completely forget and ignore their own offspring in a foreign land?

We sing, almost tearfully at times "God Bless America."

But we are almost constrained to ask: How can He?

Education In Morals

AT ONE TIME President Grant said that people cannot know about the Gospel unless they are taught it. Children are not born with a testimony of the truth, he said, any more than they are born with a knowledge of mathematics.

It is true likewise of good morals, which are an important part of the Gospel. No one can be a good Christian if he is not likewise moral. Morality and spirituality go hand in hand. Christ was our greatest teacher of good morals.

But where are morals to be taught?

Apparently drawing a line between morals and religion, the schools are prohibited from teaching religion — even offering a prayer — but they are at full liberty to discuss a subject upon which morals are based, and to do so in a manner which clearly influences morals.

The inconsistency of such a situation has never been explained.

It is admitted that children need instruction in morals, just as they need it in all phases of the Gospel of Christ.

But where is that teaching to be given?

Is it wise to give it publicly in such a way as to create a desire for corruption? Should it be taught in such a way as to invite ridicule of the foundations of good character?

Is it to be made a part of the "sex revolution" which has engulfed the world and brought about the greatest decline in morality in our age, with a plague of social disease in its wake?

Or, looking at the subject from another point of view we might ask:

Who is competent to give moral instruction to our children on a wholesome basis?

Who can teach sex without referring to the use of sex, legitimate or otherwise, without creating lust?

Does any school teacher, by reason of certification in music, mathematics or geography, automatically become qualified to teach the intricate and almost baffling subject of sex?

Because of the "sex revolution," the public mind has swung to the illicit far more than toward the virtuous. The proper teaching of sex requires the teaching of complete chastity. To vary from chastity in such instruction is to make it a course of study in sex experimentation outside the bonds of matrimony.

The experience of Sweden and other European countries clearly confirms the fact that public sex education increases promiscuity, and as promiscuity is increased, VD spreads like wildfire.

If schools are to be prohibited from teaching religion, they should be barred from destroying religion.

If schools are to be prohibited from teaching morals, they should be barred from aiding in even the least degree a destruction of morals.

If parents are not qualified to teach their children about sex, let us ask if school teachers are any better qualified. Can they uphold personal purity any better than parents?

The fact that a person becomes an educator does not make him an expert in all fields. The teachers themselves will be the first to admit that.

Sex education belongs in the home. Parents should accept their responsibility to teach chastity to their children as they reveal to them the facts of life. This is the appropriate time.

Who can better teach purity of life than a father or mother who believes that procreation is part of the divine creative work of God, and that "multiplying and replenishing the earth" therefore must be kept on a plane of spirituality and purity?

Parents can learn to teach their children. God commands them to do so. And as they teach the facts of life, they must place those facts in the proper perspective which will help youngsters to know that God has made sex pure with a divine purpose.

Movements to place sex education in nearly all grades of public schools can end only in the same result which came to Sweden. To give public sex instruction in mixed classes, and possibly by persons who may not have the highest morals themselves, is an invitation to corruption.

Sex education belongs in the home. It should be provided properly. Parents should assume this responsibility, fully and exclusively.

The "Accepted" Thing

A POET ONCE spoke of sin with the words: "First we pity, then endure, and then embrace."

This is so descriptive of present-day thinking that it is almost startling, particularly as we see so many things which the past generation regarded as debasing now being accepted as entirely proper.

As people change their standards of right and wrong, they begin to suppose that what was a sin a generation ago is no longer so, that standards are relative things which change with usage and desire, and that old-fashioned goodness now has turned into priggishness.

They actually seem to think that popularity is what determines right or wrong and that moral values change with public sentiment.

Under this kind of thinking conscience is erased and there remains only acceptance of any and all acts, no matter what they may be.

One example: A nationally circulated magazine a short time ago carried an article with the heading: "Sex is fun — Enjoy it."

Of course it said nothing of the costs of free love in venereal disease, insanity and other crippling effects of syphilis; the loss of honor, respectability, family and character. It spoke only of "enjoying wallowing in filth."

Recently a high American official quoted a European delegate to an international congress of women on the subject of illegitimate births. This delegate proudly announced that in her country there are no illegitimate children. The American official, at first thrilled at the thought of any country wiping out illegitimacy, was shocked on learning the facts. Illegitimacy there had been wiped out only by making it acceptable. The country under discussion is one in which sex freedom is the expected and accepted thing. It has been made respectable!

Extreme as this may seem, it is nonetheless representative of much of the thinking of the present day.

Styles of dress are part of this over-all pattern.

A generation ago what woman would have exposed her knees to the "admiring" public? Five years ago would any woman have exposed her thighs because it was fashionable?

Someone has said of miniskirts that they cannot get any shorter and remain skirts.

But what if they do not remain skirts? What if fashion decrees even more abbreviated costumes, will women obey and wear them? Just who is this "fashion" and what are his or her motives? Will our women consider that?

The topless craze in restaurants has now gone from coast to coast and all over Europe. Is that good or bad? Is it made good by public acceptance?

How long will police officers in beach cities continue to resist the topless swim suit trend? At first some arrests were made. Has anyone heard of any court action recently? Are we being "conditioned" to this too? Will public opinion soon require the liberalizing of laws on indecent exposure to permit this sinful fad?

A generation ago homosexuality was hardly thought of, and certainly never brought into the open. Today public opinion has been so "conditioned" to this type of moral depravity that some areas are legalizing it!

Many youths do not consider they have had an evening's date unless they have "gone all the way." And they think they can't have fun without a bottle.

This generation may rationalize itself into complete intoxication with sin, and proclaim to high heaven that it is old-fashioned to be clean, but it will yet wake up to the stern reality that God does not change, and that the moral laws are His, not man's to shift with every whim.

The divine laws on morals remain the same throughout the ages, and so do their penalties.

Adultery is still next to murder in the Lord's category of crime.

It was God who made homosexuality a capital crime in ancient Israel.

It was the Almighty who decreed in the very beginning that men and women must cover their nakedness.

No amount of rationalizing can change God's laws.

No amount of fashion designing can turn immodesty into virtue.

No amount of popularity can change sin into righteousness.

"All we like sheep have gone astray," it was once said, but those words should never describe God's kind of sheep.

Those going into the Lord's sheepfold must be Christ-like. There is nothing sacred about the world's unstable conceptions of "the accepted thing."

Where We Should Stand

THE EXPRESSION "CREDIBILITY GAP" has been widely used recently, both in prudence and in ridicule.

Far too many of our actions now bridge that gap. The circle is ever widening and the results are frightening.

One of the most incredible attitudes yet expressed comes from the mother of a girl about to enter college. She wonders if she should give her daughter a supply of "the pill" as she leaves for school. In writing to a doctor who conducts a newspaper column, she said:

"Personally I don't approve of sexual relations outside of marriage, but I wonder if I should be realistic and supply my daughter with birth-control pills just in case."

Incredible! Even that is hardly the word for it.

Can any mother in her right mind take such a position? Has she never taught her daughter the Lord's law of chastity? Why does she fear pregnancy but apparently have no fear of her daughter losing her virtue?

Can any mother be willing, "just in case," to sacrifice the morals of her child on the altar of social acceptance? Is social prestige more important than virtue? Does she have no respect for divine law?

If any mothers have so far lost their moral equilibrium that they are willing to allow their daughters to become illicit in the name of realism, what are we to expect of the girls themselves — and of the sons — and of the fathers?

Does being realistic mean that we must throw cleanliness away and become filthy because certain other people are filthy?

Do headlines on crime and sex stories so blind us that we fail to realize that there are far more clean people in the world than there are depraved ones?

Is this mother not willing to be realistic enough to admit that immorality can destroy her daughter? Why should she condone loose morals either in her child or in the school she attends?

Of course, the fact of the matter is — if we are to continue to be realistic — that too many people have lost their faith in the Source of virtue and morality — the Almighty.

When we lose faith, we certainly lose respect, and when we no longer respect the Deity it is but natural to ignore His commandments and concentrate on social allurements instead.

People who are truly realistic now recognize the existence of God more than ever before. Persons of genuine intellect, the true researchers, the great philosophers and the outstanding educators not only acknowledge but worship Him.

It is the selfish element in the world which no longer accepts the Deity. And why? Because they do not want to be interrupted in their ingrown pursuits, and are so involved in their personal desires, passions, appetites and lusts, that they have no room for sacred things. Therefore they reject or ignore God.

Of course, there are always those who are not well informed and are willing to take the word of "God-is-dead" rationalists. Such people never do think for themselves.

But to the true realist, God is a great and significant reality who guides the ultimate destiny of the world.

His most basic law concerns morality.

It is irrevocable and inescapable, and is applicable to all, whether we believe in God or not. Everyone is subject to its penalties no matter how we may try to ignore them.

The wage of sin is death — even to the unbeliever!

Immorality is next to murder in God's category of crime, and always brings its wages of destruction and remorse, even to college students who carry "the pill" with a mother's consent.

Our own nation was built upon a foundation of morality and spirituality. It is just possible that a rejection of these basic factors may bring about its fall. It was so with Greece and Rome. It can happen to us unless we repent.

Every one of us would do well to remember that the "mills of the Gods grind slowly but they grind exceeding small."

No one can flout divine law with impunity.

Every right-thinking person should be willing even to die in defense of virtue, whether that death be physical or social.

"Thou shalt not commit adultery" will forever stand as an immutable law to all human beings.

The World About Us

THE LORD HAS told the Latter-day Saints that Satan is making war against them.

He said that in this war Satan is encompassing us round about in his effort to destroy the work of God.

How does he make war with the Saints?

He does so by attacking the high ideals and sacred standards which protect our spirituality.

He encompasses us round about by encircling us with allurements and temptations which already have destroyed high standards among many people of the world, and by which he now hopes to infiltrate our ranks.

By making sin popular with the world, he hopes to make it equally popular among us.

In the world about us, high standards are falling, and lower ones — not worthy of the name — are being set up. Some efforts are being made toward no standards at all.

It is this moral breakdown that must concern the Latter-day Saints as we train the youth of the Church for their ultimate and divine destiny.

Let us look briefly at the "enemy" in this moral warfare.

The illegitimacy rate has tripled in the last ten years.

Promiscuity has increased to a point where it is thrusting upon this country a plague of social diseases.

There are more than a million new cases of V.D. in the United States each year, with 56 per cent of them being accounted for among teenagers.

Utah and Idaho are among the cleanest areas in the world in this respect.

The incidence of V.D. in the state of New York, for example, is 20 times higher than in Utah and Idaho. In Maryland it is 15 times higher, and in Florida 30 times higher.

In San Francisco, on a per capita basis, there are 30 times more cases than in Utah and Idaho; in New York City it is 40 times higher, and in the city of Newark, New Jersey, it is 100 times more.

Widespread immorality is inseparably related to the staggering increase in pornographic books, magazines, movies and TV programs which are being thrust before the public.

Pornography has become a cancerous growth which is taking a deadly toll in moral corruption in every nation in the free world.

Figures also show that most drug addicts began using narcotics as teenagers, many of them as high school students.

In the United States 4,500 children take up cigarette smoking every day. Some begin at 9 or 10 years of age, many become addicts by the time they are 14.

In a recent eastern survey conducted by Rutgers University among 17,000 students, it was revealed that from one-half to two-thirds of the students in grades 9 to 12 use alcoholic liquors.

Most young Americans get their first drinks in their own homes from their own parents.

The U.S. liquor industry has announced its objective to have at least 73 per cent of the national population as regular drinkers within the next four years.

Already 62 per cent of the adult population drink; only 38 per cent are abstainers.

The National Safety Council says that among automobile drivers responsible for accidents in California, 66 per cent had been drinking. In Florida the figure is 92 per cent.

So the world is all about us. We are "encompassed round about." To what extent will it invade our ranks?

Statistics like these are frightening indeed, but they are a necessary warning. It behooves every home to be vigilant in providing the only protection there is against such sins — a high degree of spirituality.

The Stench Of
Moral Decay

THE FOLLOWING STIMULATING editorial was published recently by the *Sacramento* (Calif.) *Union*. It so effectively sets forth one of America's greatest dangers that we reproduce it entirely below:

Entitled "Moral Decay Stench Getting Even Riper," the editorial says:

"Moral decay is as unwelcome in our society as any disease. Yet it is an unwholesome and all-too-common sight today. It is visible, in all its evil degradation, in almost every aspect of life and communications.

"In public and in private, there are few activities which have not been seduced by a permissive environment. This has unhappily led to promotion and acceptance of standards which bring out in man all that leads to excess and indulgence.

"Good taste is rudely brushed aside. The senses, which were made for the fulfillment and enjoyment of things which are beautiful, are tempted to become abused and depraved.

"There is a subversive pretense to be educational, entertaining, and instructive. The moral junk which fills so much of what is offered for reading, hearing, or viewing is an insult. It is an affront to the very spirit and meaning of man's highest endeavors.

"Instead of using the precious gifts of communication for man's betterment and true happiness, we find them overflowing with the decadence of gutter filth.

"Instead of aiming always to achieve excellence and toward helping mankind, there are those who prey like vultures on a public unfortunately only too ready to sink into the contaminated, polluted atmosphere of depravity.

"The poison of pornography is as great a menace to society today as the growing crime rate with which it is so often associated.

"From books, movies, magazines, shows, and meetings there is an overwhelming abundance of encouragement to lower standards. It is made attractive to sink into the 'accepted' and depraved ways of the pornographic promoters.

"There is so-called 'pop' art, which often is simply an excuse for utter vulgarity. There are 'love-ins' which are euphemistic cloaks for immorality.

"On all sides we are experiencing the spread of gutter filth which is passed off as 'literature.' It seduces the young and makes a mockery of the fine art of literary expression. The four-letter words and the concentration on deviant sex are excused on grounds of realism.

"Even the beauty of the ballet has been disfigured with portrayals which break the bounds of decency and make a mockery of this beautifully expressive art form.

"Movies, radio, and television, whose mass visual and audio communication should cause producers to ponder their effects, are not innocent. More and more movies stretch to the utmost the limits of decency. And sexual perverts have been featured on both radio and television as interesting interview personalities.

"We are assuredly at war today on the home front. It is a war to fight against the insidious evil of anything goes. We must re-establish moral codes and endorse them, before everything good is gone."

Is Chastity Outdated?

THE SAN FRANCISCO CHRONICLE recently carried a special column in which it published interviews with seven "people on the street."

The same question was put to all of them: "Is chastity outdated?"

All answered yes.

A merchant seaman said, "Morals have changed; virginity is on the way out. Love is in."

A furniture dealer said: "Virtue can hurt you. Virgins are really weird."

An engineer commented: "Virginity became outdated long ago. I have nothing against virginity, but in the sixties things just changed."

A psychology student answered, "Yes, morals have changed."

A hair stylist said that virtue passed out five years ago.

Another barber agreed, and said there are very few people these days who are virtuous.

These were all men. One lone girl was also asked the question, and she (pity her) agreed with the men, saying that chastity is outdated because in these enlightened days people are freer.

No one can say whether this is a fair cross-section of the thinking of San Francisco citizens, nor if it is representative of the thinking of people elsewhere.

That it is to some extent, at least, is proven by the vast increase in the prevalence of venereal disease, which is a fairly accurate barometer of the morals of the general public.

V.D., as it is called, is now considered as an epidemic out of hand. This is true in America as well as in other nations.

In the United States 1,500 teenagers catch this dread disease every day, and 1,300 adults do likewise. It is spreading fastest among teens because, as the girl explained, "we are freer."

That matter of being freer simply means to let down the bars, to throw away ideals, good character and good health. It means freer to deny God and the Ten Commandments. But is this kind of freedom desirable?

This question also may be answered in terms of V.D.

The *Chicago Tribune* reported recently that "the increasing number of gonorrhea cases has reached a point where it is now classified as an alarming epidemic." It quoted the Illinois public health office.

The newspaper went on to say that in this country ONE OUT OF EVERY 30 PERSONS IN THE 20-TO-24-YEAR AGE BRACKET NOW HAS A VENEREAL DISEASE.

Dr. Norman J. Rose, head of epidemiology for the Illinois Department of Public Health, said that "the situation in regard to gonorrhea is extremely bad and getting worse at a frightening rate."

In Illinois the cases have doubled in ten years.

Dr. Rose pointed out that the problem is worse than official figures would indicate because he said that for every case reported to doctors by infected people, there are two that go unreported.

Dr. Jack Sloan, associated with Dr. Rose, said that "contrary to the popular notion that venereal disease is no longer a menace, the U.S. Public Health Service reports: V.D. IS THE NATION'S LEADING COMMUNICABLE DISEASE." Chicago is first among all cities in the nation in the number of syphilis cases, and third in gonorrhea.

Figures sometimes do not portray the real picture. The report says that one in every 30 Americans 20 to 24 years of age has V.D. Think of that in terms of smallpox or polio. What if one in every 30 such persons in America had polio? What if that number had smallpox? What if that many had to be operated on for cancer? Wouldn't we be shaken by the very thought of it? Yet that is the condition in regard to V.D.

Syphilis is a killer; it also maims, causes heart trouble, insanity and blindness. It is the price of "being freer."

Latter-day Saints at least should know the true meaning of virtue. God's word is never passé. It is never outdated. No matter what the philosophies of men may be, God's word — for Latter-day Saints — must prevail.

No man on earth can ever cancel out the divine injunction:

"THOU SHALT NOT COMMIT ADULTERY."

The Easy Way To Live

WE OFTEN SPEAK of people who have an easy life — or a hard one — and sometimes we mention those who "come up the hard way."

It seems that some of the best people have the hardest time and that evil ones often have all the advantages in life. But is it really so?

The Lord has said that His people will be tried and even persecuted from time to time, and that they may be spoken of and dealt with in unkindly ways. This is true. Many of the great prophets were martyred.

Our own Pioneers had what many would regard as a hard life, being forced from their homes, obliged to cross plains and mountains to find a refuge, and compelled to subdue the desert to earn a living.

But was theirs a hard life? They didn't consider it so. They were builders of the Kingdom of God, and found joy in their labors. Though their toil was hard and their privations serious, in their hearts they knew the joy that comes to those who serve God and keep His commandments. It made their burdens light.

Then what is the hard life?

Some who are evil enjoy the riches of the earth — fine cars, luxurious apartments, costly vacations, even the adulation of the crowd. But is theirs the easy life?

It should be remembered that the prophet of old said there is no happiness in wickedness. As virtue is its own reward, so is sin.

To determine whether a life is hard or easy, we must merely examine the harvest it brings.

Although a saintly life filled with persecution may seem hard, it develops great faith, steadfastness of soul, and strength of character.

Did not the Savior say: "Blessed are they which are persecuted for righteousness' sake: for theirs is the kingdom of heaven"?

Let it not be supposed that they earned the Kingdom of Heaven by suffering at the hands of wicked people. They earned the Kingdom of Heaven by developing faith, character and Christ-like souls. Of course they were a blessed people, becoming so Christ-like as to be worthy of entering His Kingdom. Only the Christ-like can receive it.

There is no excellence without labor. Gold is not rendered from ore without a crucible. Even the Savior learned obedience by the things which He suffered. Suffering, exertion, patience are all part of the price of progress toward the divine.

So it is not labor which makes a life hard or easy. God expects us to labor. He told Adam and Eve that they were to live by the sweat of their face. Work is good for people. It is part of the good life.

Is the evil life really easy — this life of pleasure, indulgence and abandon?

It is indeed the hard life, for the wages of sin is death. Sometimes it is a slow death brought on by the diseases of indulgence. It includes the enmity of "crooks who catch crooks," the breakdown of home, loss of employment, and the heartaches of loved ones deeply distressed because of the prodigality of a son or daughter.

The most wretched part of a life of sin is being without God. To live without Him is the most difficult of all living. To resist Him by knowingly opposing Him is to kick against the pricks senselessly. It leads to self-destruction.

The Gospel is the greatest power known to man for the betterment of the human race. It elevates the soul, providing hope and purpose in life. To live it is intelligent, to enjoy it is to receive the choice blessings of our existence.

The Lord has said that if we will serve Him, He will open the windows of heaven and pour out such blessings that we can hardly contain them.

These blessings have only one purpose — to help us to become "like your Father which is in heaven." That is the ultimate objective of life.

The Female Of The Species

IT IS WIDELY believed that most girls and women live cleaner lives than most boys and men.

Whether this be true or not, certainly the right-thinking male rejoices in the sweetness and purity of a virtuous woman.

The strength of good motherhood has been a prime force for stability and righteousness all through history, and it will continue to be so as long as girls and women hold the line for righteousness.

But now the line begins to weaken. The trend in some areas is taking an adverse direction.

The United Press recently reported a significant increase in crime among girls and women.

It is well-known that most shoplifting is done by women and girls and that this type of crime is mounting rapidly.

Other kinds of theft over fifty dollars — not counting automobiles — are growing faster among teenage girls than among boys of the same age, according to this report.

The increase of juvenile crime last year rose twice as fast as the increase in population. A large part of it was among girls, for as the U.P.I. reports: "There was no increase in the number of juvenile cases involving boys."

However, there are still four times as many boys in juvenile court cases as there are girls.

The U.P.I. says that the juvenile delinquency rate in urban areas is three times as high as in rural areas.

Noting the increase in juvenile court cases involving girls, the United States Health, Education and Welfare Department reports:

"Almost half of all female juvenile cases handled by the courts last year involved sex-related offenses. There was also a sharp increase in juvenile drug cases where again the rate of increase for girls was half again above that for boys."

The United States Children's Bureau says that sex-related cases involving girls from ten to seventeen had increased eight per cent over the previous year. The increase in urban areas alone was 13 per cent.

Mrs. Catherine B. Oettinger, Chief of the Children's Bureau, says: "We are particularly alarmed by the fact that so large a percentage of girls are involved in sex-related offenses because they now compose almost half of all girls' delinquency cases handled by the court."

The hunger for popularity is the basis for much of the willingness to lower the bars, both for boys and girls.

"Everybody does it" is almost the univeral defense when youngsters are asked for the reason why.

And that "everybody does it" covers a wide area from miniskirts and tight clothes to drinking, smoking and petting.

But the information of these young people is wrong!

Everyone does not indulge. Everyone is not delinquent. The majority are wonderful!

It may be altogether true — and is — that within certain groups "everyone does it," but they are not representative groups.

Most young people want to be good and they are.

If anyone thinks "everybody does it" — the "it" referring to shady things — then let him open his eyes to the facts and join a new crowd where people are clean and do clean things.

Safety lies to a large extent in being with good people who do not tempt their friends.

Good people want to be with other good people because they want good activities.

We usually think of boys as the ones who should be strong, always protecting their girl friends from harm. And by all means they should be.

But it seems that many girls still can lead many boys any way they like. The girls then must be the stronger of the two.

If girls maintain their standards, the boys are more likely to follow suit, but if the girls fall they drag boys down into the depths with themselves. Girls so often forget that they have most to lose and most to pay.

Virtue is above price, but probably only those who lose it fully measure its value.

Styles And Standards

THE WAYS OF man and the ways of God are far apart and never the twain shall meet, unless man changes his ways to correspond with those of the Lord.

But willful man always has gone his own way. Only the repentant have made the adjustment.

Man's ways nearly always involve popularity. With God's path it is often quite the opposite.

Is popularity to be our measure and standard of personal conduct?

Is "but everyone does it" the controlling factor?

Can custom, style or fashion determine what is good and what is not?

Consider some of the customs and fashions of today, and what they bring to us.

Let us talk about drugs for a moment. Some reports indicate that half the high school students of the nation have experimented with them to some degree and that as many as 20 per cent of the students use them regularly.

Popularity is immediately involved. Even the youngsters who use them know that these drugs are harmful and can bring even insanity or death. And they taste bad, too.

But danger or taste to the contrary, the drugs are used because "everyone does it," not because there is anything desirable about them.

Think next of tobacco and liquor. A 15-year-old boy recently said, "I tried them both but they tasted so bad that once was enough."

But with all their dangers to health and happiness, both are used by many who think it is the thing to do to be popular, awful taste and all. It seems that some will do almost anything to be one with the crowd.

Immorality on a date is becoming "the accepted and expected thing" in some circles. This promiscuity is not only destroying the moral fibre of the nations, but it is spreading venereal disease so rapidly that public health officials now regard it as an epidemic which is out of control.

Does this "accepted thing" make it really acceptable? Can corruption be turned into goodness simply by making it popular?

One of the most notable examples of throwing standards to the winds in favor of popularity is to be found, of course, in both men's and women's styles.

Because misguided publishers and radio program planners give undue publicity to the hippie element, long hair, dirty clothes and filthy habits have appeared on nearly every campus in the country.

Can such popularity make filth and base indulgence good?

And when Paris and New York decree shorter skirts, even mothers and grandmothers expose themselves indecently because it is stylish. They should (and do) know better, which makes it even worse.

History repeats itself in these matters.

The Devil is no more changeable than is God.

Always he has told people to "believe it not" when the sacred word has been preached. Always he has tempted them to sin. Always he has deceived them and made them think that if it glitters, and if he makes it popular, even sin will become acceptable.

But always God has held fast, and has commanded His people to observe His standards.

And always also, even some of His Saints have tried to compromise and serve two masters.

Can we really afford to be "right with fashion" when it makes us wrong with God?

The Devil Is A Liar

THE SCRIPTURES TEACH that the Devil is a liar, and has been from the beginning.

But he is not the only one, for he endeavors to persuade all else to become like himself. With many he succeeds abundantly, much to his own gratification.

In speaking of this propensity, the Lord says of the Devil:

"He saith unto them: Deceive and lie in wait to catch, that ye may destroy; behold, this is no harm. And thus he flattereth them, and telleth them that it is no sin to lie that they may catch a man in a lie, that they may destroy him.

"And thus he flattereth them, and leadeth them along until he draggeth their souls down to hell; and thus he causeth them to catch themselves in their own snare." (D&C 10:25-26.)

Since dishonesty, insincerity and a passion to "save face" have become such a part of our modern way of life, this scripture brings a timely warning.

As criminality has soared tremendously in the recent past, so has lying to cover up dishonesty.

Deceit, wearing a false front, misrepresentation of facts, and scheming for our own aggrandizement, are all part of the same package.

Lying is as despicable as is stealing. Often they are the same, for in lying, people's good names are often stolen away. It is a vicious form of character assassination.

This is particularly true in such cases as are referred to in the above mentioned scripture, where people tell lies in an effort to destroy another person.

Murder is a crime for which there is no forgiveness. How near to it is character assassination?

And yet, how many ostensibly respectable people indulge in it!

Let us ask ourselves frankly: If no unclean thing can enter the Kingdom of Heaven, can a liar do so? Is he clean? Is there anything pure or Christ-like about him — or her?

We might well remember the eternal place to which the Lord says liars will go — if unrepentant:

"These are they who are liars, and sorcerers, and adulterers, and whoremongers, and whosoever loves and makes a lie.

"These are they who suffer the wrath of God on earth. These are they who suffer the vengeance of eternal fire. These are they who are cast down to hell." (D&C 76:103-106.)

Whenever people lie or even color the truth, they place themselves in league with the Devil, and he is hardly good company for the Saints.

How different is the liar from the true Saint, who endeavors to exemplify the teachings of Christ! How different are his — or her — motives!

The true Saint is one who loves his neighbor as himself, who does unto others as he would be done by; it is he who judges not, that he may not be judged; it is he who is forgiving and kind, patient and long suffering; it is he who seeks a friendly reconciliation with his brother with whom he may have a difference, and does so even before he comes to worship at the altar of God.

The Saint is a good Samaritan, not a robber on the road to Jericho. The Saint will go the extra mile and give his cloak and his coat also, but will never steal another's cloak, and certainly not his good name.

The Saint will know that unless he loves his brother whom he has seen, he obviously does not love God whom he has not seen. He forgives, but does not condemn — he helps, but never hinders — he holds out a light that others may see, but never blinds them.

So strongly does the Lord feel on this matter of lying that He has said:

"These six things doth the Lord hate: yea, seven are an abomination unto him:

"A proud look, a lying tongue, and hands that shed innocent blood, an heart that deviseth wicked imaginations, feet that be swift in running to mischief, a false witness that speaketh lies, and he that soweth discord among brethren." (Proverbs 6.)

The Battle For Virtue

THERE IS NO place for complacency when a serious conflict involves us.

To say that "all is well in Zion" is but to deceive ourselves, as the Book of Mormon so clearly teaches.

As long as there is a vigorous campaign to destroy chastity, no Latter-day Saint can sit by and say "all is well in Zion." And such a campaign is under way.

It is not only directed at Latter-day Saints, it is nationwide, worldwide, and we are but a single segment of the world. But it will hit us as hard as anyone unless we are on guard.

Consider for a moment some of the forces arrayed against virtue:

1—Among us we have a legal battle over the display and distribution of smut among our young people. The community of Provo, for example, passed an ordinance to control pornography. One man and a lawyer blocked the city in its efforts. The majority does not rule. The vast majority wants this smut eliminated from the city. But one man and a lawyer stand in the way. And what does smut do to chastity?

2—Atheistic movements are gaining ground among us as elsewhere. Some professors in school take delight in destroying faith, and nothing is done about it. The

"God is dead" philosophy is stimulated by clergymen who have become disgusted with dead forms in their own churches and feel that if this is all religion has to offer then it is not worth while. Dead forms are killing what religion is left in many churches. But how does this affect chastity? It removes the restraints that religion alone can place upon immorality. Loss of faith goes hand in hand with loss of virtue.

3—Legislatures are beginning to relax moral laws relating not only to adulterous relationships but also to homosexuality and prostitution. What is wrong with a lawmaker who condones homosexuality? What is wrong with a lawmaker who condones prostitution to the point where he will work to make it legal for a 16-year-old child to become a commercial harlot? And what is wrong with citizens who elect such lawmakers?

4—Current dating practices among many young people promote lust. Setting aside standards which seem no longer sacred to them, many youngsters go the limit for the sake of popularity, for a thrill, or to show their independence. Nationwide the result is that — in spite of "the pill" and other preventatives — one out of every 14 babies born in America is illegitimate. Serious as this is, it does not indicate the number of illicit contacts made where no pregnancy occurs.

5—Promiscuity is growing so fast in America that it has brought a wave of social disease which not only blinds and cripples thousands every year, but actually kills a thousand people every month.

6—Dating is developing among married people, and this kind of conduct is not ordinary partying. It represents the worst, and is becoming an increasingly important cause of divorce.

7—The introduction of contraceptives on a wide scale, making them available to the unmarried as well

as to the married, and the encouragement of the use
of these devices by great governments, including our
own, is becoming one of the greatest of all threats to
morality.

8—Glorifying lustfulness in movies, making it seem
desirable and not sinful, cloaking with respectability
theatrical people who encourage seduction in the minds
of their audiences, contribute to an acceptance of low
moral standards or none at all.

Many more factors might be mentioned. But simply stated, the fact is that immorality is increasing
rapidly. It is invading our communities, breaking down
the standards of some of our own people, and is a potent threat to the very souls of our children.

We are Latter-day Saints. But to be Latter-day Saints
indeed, we must live the laws of God, foremost among
which is the law of chastity.

Without chastity we are not true Latter-day Saints.
Without chastity there is no salvation. Immorality is
apostasy from the teachings of Christ. Apostasy leads
to destruction of the soul, and this particular type of
apostasy leads to destruction of the body as well.

Our whole purpose in being members of the Church
is to save our souls. Now that the forces of evil — particularly of unchastity — are so prevalent and so potent, can we remain complacent as they threaten the
actual reason for our membership in God's holy Church?

Dare we stand by and see our youngsters destroy
themselves morally and physically?

We must exert every necessary effort to save them
in our communities, in our homes and in the Church.

We must once again enthrone virtue in its proper
place, and remember that there is no salvation, no happiness and no progress without it. And we must remember too that in stark reality, the wages of sin is
DEATH.

Can God's Laws Be Outmoded?

RECENTLY THE AUTHOR of a book which seeks to persuade legislators to legalize moral perversions listed a set of reasons why he thought the laws of the land should be liberalized to remove all stigma from moral corruption.

One of his principal arguments was:

"Most of the commands of God are now obsolete and people no longer find it necessary to obey them."

He then went on to talk about the destruction of Sodom and Gomorrah as an "old wives' tale conveniently ignored by all in modern times." The book then goes on to say that "man can be either homosexual, heterosexual or bi-sexual — the choice is his."

Most people who commit serious sin attempt to justify their acts. The perverts of the world are now attempting to do that publicly. For many years — even for generations — this particular type of sinner has been willing to remain in darkness of his own choosing and cover his shame with secrecy.

This is no longer the case. Deviates now are proud of their "profession" and openly advertise it. Brashly and blatantly they demand their place in the sun, and insist upon being regarded as respectable, both under the law and in society at large.

They have become far more numerous than we might suppose. There are literally millions of them in the United States, not to mention those living in other parts of the world. In America they are now organized into groups through which they hope to achieve social acceptance and political strength sufficient to relax the laws against them.

In their struggle they seek to prove that their perversions are not sins, but natural tendencies which should be recognized and accepted. Hence they say that since God's laws are now obsolete, their acts are no longer sinful, and therefore not to be looked down upon.

Few of these deviates will ever be drawn back into a chaste society. Few if any have such a desire. They like their life, they love darkness better than light, and are content to remain so — except that they are no longer willing to carry a stigma, the mark of the unclean.

How utterly blind they are! And how gullible are those who sympathize with the idea that deviates were born with these tendencies, and therefore should be accepted as they are!

And how blind are those who suppose that God's laws are outmoded, and no longer in force!

What these foolish individuals do not seem to know is that God's laws are binding whether mankind chooses to ignore them or not, and they cannot escape the penalties of their own misdeeds. The wheels of the Gods may grind very slowly, but inevitably they grind exceedingly small.

It is not that God sets out deliberately to bring unhappiness upon these much-to-be-pitied but headstrong deviates. They bring upon themselves the wages of their own sins. And then at last, in the depths of suffering from which only death can release them, they cry out and defy a Deity who would be so cruel and heartless as to punish them in such a way!

God's laws never change. "It is easier for heaven and earth to pass, than one tittle of the law to fail," the Savior said.

And this is so. Experience demonstrates it day by day. No one can fly in the face of Providence with impunity. No matter how much they deny God, their denials will not exterminate Him. God lives, and still controls the universe. The laws of nature — and of sex — are immutable and unfailing. Death will still continue to be the final wage of sin. Life and joy are the rewards of righteousness.

Sex is for the procreation of the species, not for sensual pleasure. God made it clean and sacred. He intends that we shall keep it so.

And why do we write in this way about deviates and their peculiar notions? For two reasons:

First, to say to them, and to all other unbelievers, that "God is not dead, nor doth He sleep."

Second, to remind all Latter-day Saints that chastity is more important to us than mortal life, and that as the bearers of the vessels of the Lord, we must be clean — clean as the angels, remembering the divine injunction:

"Keep thy father's commandment, and forsake not the law of thy mother:

"Bind them continually upon thine heart, and tie them about thy neck.

"When thou goest, it shall lead thee; when thou sleepest, it shall keep thee; and when thou wakest, it shall talk with thee.

"For the commandment is a lamp; and the law is light; and reproofs of instruction are the way of life." (Proverbs 6.)

Have We The Courage?

How much courage does the average Latter-day Saint have? Enough to stand by his convictions?

If brought to the test, how strong will he be?

This is no academic question. Actually it comes to the very heart of a situation which now confronts us, for the test is here and we are in the process of reacting to it.

Today's greatest challenge to our way of life is the world-wide assault upon chastity. Immorality is becoming an acceptable — even a respectable — way of life in the world.

While Sweden admits to 80 per cent promiscuity among its young people, and this without condemnation from its national leaders, that country is not alone.

Others are no doubt equally guilty, but they neither admit it nor do they advertise it. Yet research shows the condition is there.

Fortunately, America is among the cleanest of them all, for which we are most thankful. But this promised land has more than it should have of this condition and the situation here is becoming worse.

This world-wide attack upon chastity has many facets, all of which converge on the one point: The destruction of virtue.

What are these facets?

One of the most widespread is our manner of dress, with its direct emphasis on sex appeal, and when we use that expression, we have in mind its literal connotation — an appeal to the sex urge.

Mothers and daughters alike bow to the dictum of fashion. They may or may not realize what they do, but let it be understood plainly that abbreviated, revealing clothing has the base appeal for which it is deliberately designed.

Another facet is the teaching of "new morality" which in fact is immorality, a liberty-giving invitation to promiscuity.

How great will be the condemnation of those who trap others with their flouting of the divine law against unchastity!

Another is the present unwise practice of dating among youth, beginning at an early age, leading to intimacies of varying degrees.

Popular customs in partying by married people who close their eyes to their wedding vows is a rapidly growing phase of this corrupting over-all attack upon virtue.

Liquor, tobacco, and certain drugs have a demoralizing effect on character and tend to lower the bars and open the floodgates to sin. Why do we fail to recognize this? Why do so many love darkness rather than light?

The pressure for public sex education is another facet of this situation. Surely Americans should be willing to learn from others, and in this instance from the Swedes whose ten years of sex education now have made so much of the nation promiscuous.

And then there is the frightening, continuing assault in the form of so-called entertainment, in TV, in movie films, in the drama and in the printed page.

It is amazing that respected and legitimate publishing houses stoop to the publication of books and magazines so filthy that decent-minded people must return them to the dealers, their sensibilities having been grossly insulted by what those pages contained.

There is the tendency in advertising to put seductive pictures in sales displays, in no way related to the products they attempt to sell. Why do they do it?

Under the mistaken notion that the seductive approach may enlarge their market for anything from ties to orange juice, they resort to sex as a gimmick which they believe will most quickly draw the public eye and enrich their purses.

Because the gullible are fast being educated to the "glorification" of sex, some merchants feel fully justified in exploiting it to their own profit.

Now what is to be the position of Latter-day Saints?

To what extent are we to become parties to it all?

President McKay has taught us that the first and most important duty of our people is to teach Christ and Him crucified, which includes a firm advocacy of the principles for which Jesus stands.

There is nothing more basic in all His teachings than chastity. He places unchastity next to murder in the category of crime.

Then can we as a people do less?

Can we then tolerate the insidious influences which break down chastity?

If we say no to this question, then have we the courage to take the necessary stand for Christ and His position in this matter?

Do our women and girls have the courage to create a style of their own, representative of Latter-day Saint ideals? We challenge them to do so!

Do our married couples have the courage to eschew infidelity in all its forms, even to the slightest suggestion of evil? We challenge them to do so!

Do our youth have the courage to put dating on a sensible basis which will encourage, promote and protect the virtue which is so vital to their well-being? We challenge them to do so!

Do young and old alike have the courage to put out of their lives the liquor, tobacco and other elements of the modern "social" life which are so conducive to an over-all moral breakdown? We challenge them to do so!

Will Latter-day Saints take a truly Christian attitude on sex education and keep it within the protective portals of the home where it belongs, giving to our young people the sacred point of view on procreation? We challenge them to do so!

Will every Latter-day Saint have the foresight to refuse to patronize any kind of entertainment which has an evil intent and a degrading theme? We challenge them to stand by the teachings of Christ on moral cleanliness and stay out of the habitation of the wicked!

As true followers of Christ, have we the courage to fight the pornographic literature trade and keep out of our communities the vile publications which seek to seduce our youth? We challenge every clean-minded person to do so, militantly and unhesitatingly!

We challenge every true follower of Christ to obey Him, uphold His standards and be clean.

As bearers of the vessels of the Lord, can we do less?

The Miniskirts

THE MINISKIRT WAS a British creation. At first it drew the unanimous scorn of the fashion experts in Europe and the United States.

Particularly were the French designers outspoken in their condemnation of the new fad. They pointed out that such styles threw women's clothes out of proper proportion and therefore were evidence of bad designing. Then they pointed to the ugliness of knees in general and of the fat ones and the bony ones in particular. Are there any others?

They explained that "thigh-high" dresses not only were unbecoming but distasteful, and approached the indecent. They said that no woman can be at her best in such a skirt. That was two years ago. Then they saw the financial advantage of making skirts from a minimum of material while charging a full price.

The miniskirt swept Europe, and before the French designers could catch their breath (after decreeing that hem lines should drop below the knee) the mini variety was being worn by half the girls in Paris.

Americans scoffed at it for quite some time too, but here, as in Paris, the London styles swept everything before them, and many of our women now feel obliged not only to display their badly shaped knees, but their thighs as well.

Some of the finest blood on earth came out of Britain, and some of the highest principles of justice and freedom.

Where would we be without the Magna Carta? Where would we be without the standards set for years by the great parliamentarians of that great nation? And where would we be as a Church without the thousands of valiant converts who accepted the Gospel at a time when such strength as only they could give was required for the survival of the Church?

But as it is elsewhere, not everything that comes out of England is good, and one can hardly say that the "mini-craze" has made any wholesome contribution to the attractive appearance of the feminine form, nor to the strength of a skidding morality.

Who likes miniskirts? The men? The women? The teenagers?

Not clean-minded men who are thoroughly disgusted by a display of feminine charm (?) so generously exhibited when the mini-skirted girl takes her seat or crosses her legs.

Not wholesome young boys either, who are fighting to keep their minds off sex in this day when even a real estate agent advertises "sexy apartments" as a means of leasing his property. Not decent youngsters who are fighting a world trend to destroy good morals.

Not Church leaders who are constantly appealing for modesty in dress and protection of moral standards, and who — even in Church — must stand the effrontery of women and girls who brazenly expose themselves in the sacred portals of a chapel.

Not women who are willing to look at other women and suddenly acquire the gift to see themselves as others see them.

And what about teenagers?

They are but the products of the age in which they live. When they were little children they were dressed in skirts that resembled ballet clothes. Even in winter they went bare-legged while their heads and shoulders were covered in woolens. They grew up in mini clothes. They don't know any better, because that is the way their mothers dressed them from earliest childhood.

That is the kind of clothes they wear in school gymnasiums too, where mini uniforms are all the regulations allow. Of course they cannot exercise properly if inhibited by clothes that cover their nakedness!

And what about the young marrieds? They must appear as young as the teenagers. It would not do for anyone to guess that they are "old married people." So to look as young as teenagers, they dress as if they were the same age.

Isn't it time for our women to decide to use their own good sense in regard to dress, and refuse to be like sheep following the dictates of fashion designers who like extremes?

And if they follow fashion designers, why not the French ones who decreed — but now in vain, alas! — that hemlines should go below the knee? Why not assist them to make decent styles popular?

And anyway, why shouldn't Latter-day Saints just decide to forget the world — and not be so much OF the world — and dress beautifully in becoming clothes that preserve the decency which the Lord expects of His lovely daughters?

And God Clothed Them

THE LORD INTENDED that people should wear clothing, and that such clothing should "cover their nakedness."

Indecent exposure is condemned in the scripture, while purity of mind and body are constantly stressed.

It was the Lord, in the first place, who provided that His children should wear proper clothing, and when He spoke to the Prophet Joseph Smith about our apparel, He commanded: "Let all things be done in cleanliness before me."

But clothing — to be clean — must be more than "laundry-fresh." It must be decent as well.

The Lord commanded that we love Him with all our hearts and with all our minds.

We cannot love God with an impure mind. No unclean thing can stand in His presence. We invite the Holy Spirit to come upon us, but if we have unclean minds He cannot accept our invitation.

Clean minds are a necessary prerequisite to clean hearts, and certainly have a relationship to decent dress.

As styles become less and less modest, and more and more seductive, will the people of God continue to adopt them in the face of the divine command to be clean?

For some reason respectable people seem not to realize that they themselves are caught in this wave of indecency when they surrender to the dictates of fashion and wear whatever the world wears because they do not wish to seem conspicuous.

How far shall we go in being "of the world"?

Latter-day Saints should recognize that the present trend toward revealing clothing is but a part of a world-wide movement to destroy morals. Regardless of some protestations to the contrary, there is such a movement.

Think of some of its facets:

There is the "new morality" widely heralded. It advocates unrestricted indulgence.

There are the "sex revolutions" on some high school and college campuses.

It is becoming more and more common for unmarried couples to go together on unchaperoned vacations where they travel virtually as man and wife.

Dating by many now involves going "all the way" as a matter of routine.

The "pill" is being distributed to youngsters far more widely than anyone is willing to admit.

We have the topless craze, now spreading also more than we care to acknowledge.

Some states and some nations are liberalizing laws on morality, condoning homosexuality and legalizing prostitution for 16-year-olds.

And then the styles! Tight-fitting, abbreviated and revealing! They prescribe skirts that do not allow even a mature woman to be seated and retain her modesty.

All these and more have arisen during the same period of time. And some of our people have followed them. Most of our women have adopted these styles because they say they don't want to appear conspicuous.

But why not be conspicuous in defending decency?

The fact is that many bear testimony of Christ, pledging to keep His commandments, and yet refuse to maintain our standards of modesty.

One is moved to ask: Which is stronger, our faith or our slavery to fashion?

Modesty can be achieved in stylish clothing that is both decent and becoming. There is a happy medium, and it can be achieved and enjoyed. Many are the modest women of our land who have the courage and good taste to be decent and who still retain their attractive appearance. Shall we not all do the same?

It is time to take a stand for decency and for Christ. They do go together. There is no cleanliness without decency, and the followers of the Lord must be clean.

"Let all things be done in cleanliness before me."

Time For Style
Of Our Own

THE PROPHETS OF old have long referred to the Saints of God as a "peculiar people."

What does "peculiar" mean?

It is true that most people think of it in terms of "queer," "strange" or "unusual." But like many English words, this one has other definitions, and the "strange" one is but minor in the dictionary.

The important meanings of the word are listed as: distinctive, special, individual, exclusive, independent, unlike others, privileged, having to do with private ownership.

Some of the persecution of the past as endured by the "Mormon" people has resulted from their being looked upon as queer, odd, or strange. But as the world becomes acquainted with us it now catches the vision of the true meaning of the word "peculiar" when referring to us.

We are peculiar in the distinctive sense of the word in our Welfare Program. We take care of our own. For this we receive nothing but admiration. People recognize us as being different from the rest of the world in this matter, but instead of regarding us as being "odd" they admire us for it, and wish all people would do as well.

We have been considered "queer" because we do not smoke, drink, nor otherwise abuse our bodies. That has been considered "odd" and prudish in the past, but no more. Now only respect comes from those who know us as abstainers. Many have wished they had the strength to do as well.

They don't think we are odd. They admit we are smart!

We have been looked upon for years as peculiar in the "different" sense of the word, because we live the law of tithing. But now churches throughout the world would gladly discard their collection plates for the much more remunerative system of tithing. Many denominations have done so and now invite their people to pay tithing. No longer are we considered queer on this point, either. Again, they think we are superior.

Our young people were once looked upon as oddities because they give up school, scholarships, job inducements, and the "wild oats of youth" to fill missions.

But now large companies place a premium on our returned missionaries and try to hire them, knowing that they are superior in most respects. Our missionaries are admittedly among the finest scholars at many universities. Their clean living and high character have now placed them in the much-to-be-desired distinctive class, far removed from the oddities.

Is there any reason why our girls and women cannot become equally distinctive, special, and independent, by adopting a style of their own in dress? It could be as becoming as anything Paris can produce, and yet preserve modesty and decency.

Now that styles have become "pornographic" in their suggestiveness, is it not time for Latter-day Saints to put decency above fashion, and decide to be beautifully feminine, but still remain becomingly modest?

This they may do regardless of what style-makers in Paris, London and New York decree in their effort to indecently expose the feminine form to create a sex appeal which can lead only to moral degradation.

We are two and a half million strong. No group of that size can take a united stand on an important subject without making a marked impression on the world.

A united stand for decency in dress would bring to us at least as much admiration as have our Welfare Program and our stand on the Word of Wisdom.

And it would be cheered by right-thinking men and women everywhere.

Modesty is never unbecoming. Decency is never a handicap. But both are within the scope of the laws of God.

No woman looks as lovely as when she is properly and fully clothed. What woman can suppose that ugly knees and bony shoulder blades can add luster to her charm?

If we make a style of our own, with the strength of two and a half million people to popularize it, the world will come marching to our feet and admire our courage as they now admire what we do in other ways.

It is true that we would be even more peculiar — but distinctively, specially, and gloriously so. And everyone would love it!

From Baldwin, Michigan, comes the following U.P.I. news item:

> In the day of the mod, the mini, the pop and the twig, some girls at Baldwin High School have developed a style of their own.
>
> It's mod, all right — modest.
>
> Ten girls showed up for classes in skirts that had hemlines four inches below the knee. In addi-

tion, they wore loose-fitting blouses with long sleeves and high neck lines.

The counter mod movement was started by Thyra Sweet of nearby Beitly.

"We are tired of being embarrassed by showing so much," she told her mother recently. "We are tired of tight fits and we are tired of looking at girls with knobby knees. We like long dresses."

Have Latter-day Saint girls and women the courage to do as well?

Worship Of The Body

WORSHIP IS A sacred word. It should be used only with reference to the Deity, who is the personification of purity and all things good.

But evil forces and false gods have been worshipped from the beginning, and all such worship has been disastrous.

In the days of ancient Greece and Rome there were many kinds of worship. They had false gods and corrupt philosophies, and one of them was the worship of the body.

They glorified it first in athletics. Then the emphasis shifted to the arts, and to physical urges which brought both these nations down into the morass of immorality, finally destroying them.

The world today is following this identical pattern. The body is being glorified in the minds of many, both in athletics and in aesthetics, both heading toward immorality.

Whereas Romans and Greeks seemed to put more emphasis on the male physique, we now do the opposite, making the trend more hazardous.

The Greeks at first chose physical culture as one of the great objectives of their day, but the fact that such emphasis was placed upon the body led them to sinful uses of it.

We currently follow a more dangerous course. To display the female form as is done today, stimulates the sex urge more than was the case with the Greeks. Women usually are not the aggressors in sex-sin. The reaction of men and boys is alarming!

To flagrantly display the almost nude feminine form, as is done in many of our activities, is but to invite the sexual corruption which already has become almost epidemic in every nation.

Why are women's current styles adopted? To emphasize sex.

Why do business houses adopt the sex appeal to sell tires, refrigerators, stoves, automobiles and clothing? Because the emphasis on sex seems to sell anything — from cars to refrigerators, reflecting the state of the public mind.

Is the so-called "new morality" anything other than free love? It is part of the "glorification" of the body as a fun device.

Why the hippie movement? It is largely associated with sex urges and their associated corruption.

Why the wave of pornography in films, the printed page and TV? Because sex appeal has become "sure-fire" business success for the producers.

Anciently the direct result of worship of the body was social disease. It is the same today.

Statistics from Texas, for example, should give pause to the whole nation. A United Press International dispatch from Austin recently said that more Texans die of syphilis than from tetanus, polio, diphtheria and malaria combined. The number of deaths from measles and whooping cough together are only one-third of the deaths from syphilis.

The number of cases of gonorrhea in that state is second only to "strep" throat infections, running about 800 cases a week.

A thousand Americans die every month from the effects of syphilis. Fifteen hundred youngsters between 15 and 20 years of age contract it every day, while there are 1,300 new cases daily among adults.

Syphilis causes heart trouble, crippling, insanity and blindness as well as death. The United States government spends 80 million dollars a year for the care and prevention of social disease, but can work only with known cases. Most cases are never reported. The spread has reached epidemic form.

When will we waken to our true situation? We shut our eyes to the deadly effects of tobacco, and go on smoking.

We refuse to consider the evil results of drinking liquor, and go on drinking.

And now we blissfully close our eyes to the lethal effects of our emphasis on sex.

And we are supposed to be living in an enlightened age! And we are. That is the pitiful part of it. We have the information about all these things, but are so determined to "have fun" that we forget the true source of joy, mistakenly thinking that fun is to be found in filth.

The worship of the body will bring to the modern world what it brought to Greece and Rome. We seem to love darkness more than light, and will have to endure the consequences.

A Do-It-Yourself Project

WHAT IS AS potent as fashion?

Does anything command a following to compare with it?

Fashion becomes world-wide almost over night. Although individual touches may differ, the over-all pattern of dress becomes universal, and people feel conspicuous if they are not in line.

The Orient has taken over Western styles for both men and women. French styles have become world-wide. New York creations are seen the world around. London, too, sets criteria to be followed by millions.

What is as potent as fashion?

But even fashion gets out of line at times, as do most other things. And fashion is in that position today.

In the Church we constantly speak of modesty. Our women particularly are conscious of the problem, but they feel caught between two fires — the demand for modesty on one hand, and the dictates of fashion on the other. What are they to do?

One thoughtful correspondent writes:

"You aren't the first to harp on the fashion of women's dresses. In every meeting we go to, be it Sunday School or Mutual, some one is hammering at us to keep our dresses down.

"Have you tried to buy a dress this year? I bought five for my 14-year-old girl for school. We let the hem out on all of them, and they are still too short. We went through ———'s store last Friday. You should go and take a look. The clothes on the models are from four to six inches above the knees.

"We have shopped at (and here she names five stores) etc., etc., and they are all the same — short, short, short, and no hems.

"And in the summer! Just try to find a dress, let alone sports wear, with a sleeve in!

"If we are strong enough to make our own fashions and styles, where are they? I work, and don't have time to do all of our sewing, though this seems to be the only answer.

"Since this is such a big issue of the day, can you help us instead of condemning us, especially when we have no choice from which to make our selections?"

She then makes reference to an address by one of the General Authorities in which he asks:

"Has not the time arrived when our girls and women must place decency above fashion? Cannot two and a half million people popularize decency by a united effort?"

What is the answer?

Obviously the styles are pointing to shorter and shorter skirts, not longer ones. From time to time the newspapers carry articles saying that hemlines will drop, but they never do. They seem only to rise to the point where some now are as much as eight inches above the knee, almost suggesting that skirts may soon go out of style altogether.

If this is the trend, are decent women to succumb?

Our women say that they cannot find clothing of respectable length in the stores.

If enough women demanded them, the stores would stock them!

For profit reasons, the stores will sell anything the public demands. Our merchants are not dictators. They follow the crowd just as other people do.

It is for the "crowd" to make demands on the stores. Maybe the "crowd" will have to organize for such an effort, and develop enough sentiment to make their feelings felt. We organize for political purposes, for labor reasons, and to market our crops. Why not organize for decency?

Should there be any hesitancy on the part of righteous women of all faiths to thus assert themselves? Most women are good, clean and decent. They want modesty. But they feel that they are trapped by a world movement which they cannot fight. Singly they can't but united they can and should.

Of course, as the author of the above letter indicated, it may be that women and girls will have to become pioneers again and resume the sewing of their own clothes. But is that bad? Our mothers and grandmothers did it successfully. Why not the women of today?

And if enough women began withdrawing their support from the ready-to-wear departments to make their own clothes, the stores would very quickly cooperate, even if they had to start a "do-it-yourself" project of their own.

The Rumors -- And Gossip

"LET HIM WHO is without sin first cast a stone at her."

When the Savior spoke those words he put all mankind on notice that none is perfect, not one.

But he also taught that we have no right to expose the weaknesses of another by maliciously pointing a finger of scorn and denunciation.

Who can judge his fellowman?

Who is so fair, so fully informed, and knows so well the depths of the heart as to see the intent and purpose of another's acts?

Who can sit in the scorner's seat?

And who can say like the Pharisee: "I thank thee that I am not as other men . . ."

The fact of the matter is that none is so righteous that he can regard himself as better than his fellows.

It is verily true that "there is so much good in the worst of us and so much bad in the best of us that it ill-behooves any of us to talk about the rest of us."

Then why do we so talk?

Most of the gossip that is bandied about is made up in large measure of untruths or half-truths. Most of it is repeated with some degree of malice or self-righteousness.

When the Lord has talked about gossip He usually has associated it with a "lying tongue."

This He did in Proverbs, sixth chapter, as He said:

"These six things doth the Lord hate: yea, seven are an abomination unto him:

"A proud look, a lying tongue, and hands that shed innocent blood,

"An heart that deviseth wicked imaginations, feet that be swift in running to mischief,

"A false witness that speaketh lies, and he that soweth discord among brethren."

Most gossip is at least secondhand. Most gossips have no firsthand information. They are usually rumormongers, and as such some become character assassins. Who has the right to blacken the name of anyone?

A lying tongue — wicked imaginations — running to mischief — false witness — speaking lies — sowing discord — all of these the Lord condemns as abominations.

And who can be saved in His Holy Presence if he persistently does any of these things?

Where is there place in heaven for character assassins?

Where in holy places is there room for those who speak lies and whose feet are swift in running to mischief?

Who can partake worthily of the Sacrament of the Lord's Supper while devising wicked imaginations against his neighbor?

Who can pray with sincerity to a God who denounces the constant practice of bearing false witness?

Who can build spirituality while dealing in what God hates?

And who is worthy of the name of Latter-day Saint, who is not willing to help his brother, rather than to start a whispering campaign against him?

It is interesting that in this quotation from Proverbs the Lord includes the evils of gossiping in the same passage in which He speaks of those who shed innocent blood!

There have been times when men have sacrificed their blood to preserve their good name.

If we are true followers of Christ, what will our attitude be toward our brothers and sisters?

Will it not be one of kindness and forgiveness, of protecting the unfortunate, of defending those who are wronged?

Who, if not the Latter-day Saints, should be good Samaritans?

And as such, is it not as important to bind up the wounds in a good name attacked by gossip, as to bind up the physical wounds of one attacked by thieves?

Is there a worse thief than one who steals another's good name?

It is difficult to be a true follower of Christ and forget what he said in the Sermon on the Mount:

"Judge not, that ye be not judged.

"For with what judgment ye judge, ye shall be judged: and with what measure ye mete, it shall be measured to you again.

"And why beholdest thou the mote that is in thy brother's eye, but considerest not the beam that is in thine own eye?"

Gossip, to say the least, is hardly Christ-like.

The Revulsion Has Come!

WE AMERICANS TAKE pride in the fact that in many respects we lead the world in various phases of life, and particularly in scientific and business advancement.

But there are some things in which we may well take a leaf from the books of other nations.

Great Britain, for instance, has led out far beyond American efforts in combating the evils of tobacco as it affects public health. It has also been much more forthright in its attack upon social diseases resulting from immorality.

Now it is stepping ahead of Uncle Sam in a fight against pornography.

Granted that pornography has been openly permitted in Britain for a longer period of time than has been the case in America, unconsciously enough we Americans have followed the precise pattern of pornography in England.

The British allowed pornographic books and films to go uncontrolled, as the Americans seem to be doing. But now they have had enough of it, and realize what a curse it has become to the citizenry at large.

It took a series of particularly cruel murders to bring them to their senses. Will this be necessary in our country as well?

Pornography went its filthy way in Britain until fairly recently when suddenly the newspapers announced the brutal murders of several little girls. They were torture murders involving horrible sex atrocities. As Scotland Yard went to work on the cases, they at last traced all of these crimes to one man whom they apprehended and convicted.

But in doing so, what did they also discover? That all of the crimes were experiments by the criminal in proving or disproving what he had read about in pornographic books which were sold on the public newsstands in Great Britain. He picked out young teenage victims one by one, enticed them to lonely places, and then tortured them to death while giving vent to his vicious sex perversions.

The newspapers began a campaign to stop the cause of these murders. Parliament passed laws to control pornography. The right-thinking element of Great Britain is now determined to "fight to the finish" the indecency in the printed word and in movies such as those that brought about these murders.

The pity of it is, though, that the loss of morals, in which pornography has played such an important part, now has gone so far that it may take a new generation to correct it.

The experience of Great Britain puts into stark relief the position of many of our public servants in America who, in the name of liberty, insist on giving pornography free rein.

The British at first took that position, too. No one loves independent behavior any more than an Englishman, and no one will fight an infringement of his rights any more than will a Briton.

Permitting complete abandon on the part of the makers of evil books and pictures, at first believed to be an expression of free speech and press, now is discovered to be quite the opposite.

Now it is learned so painfully that free publication of pornography is like free use of firearms in a robbery. Instead of giving complete liberty, restriction is now seen to be the need — as a means of protecting the public welfare. So now Britain has written laws to protect its public against the kind of destructive influences which brought about the horror murders of several little girls.

They announced in the press: "The revulsion has come! The tide is turned."

Now if only America, in its pride, would follow suit! If only America would recognize pornography for what it is and what it does, it might yet be that we may save the morals of young and old alike from this vicious attack by people whose only aim is to make money at the expense of the unsuspecting public.

Public officials should see this problem in its true light. They should give us at least as much protection against the peddlers of smut as they now give against the gun-wielding highwayman.

Smut's Part In Crime

THE FACT THAT smut is the leading cause of the sky-rocketing crime wave in America is strongly set forth by J. Edgar Hoover, head of the FBI.

Writing in "FBI Law Enforcement Bulletin," and reprinted in the *U.S. News and World Report,* Mr. Hoover says in part:

"The publication and sale of obscene material is BIG business in America today. Degenerate sex pictures and pornographic literature, covertly peddled and sold in most cities and communities, net greedy smut merchants millions of dollars annually.

"It is impossible to estimate the amount of harm to impressionable teen-agers and to assess the volume of sex crimes attributable to pornography, but its influence is extensive.

"Sexual violence is increasing at an alarming pace. Many parents are deeply concerned about conditions which involve young boys and girls in sex parties and illicit relations.

"While there is no official yardstick with which to measure accurately the reasons for increases in any criminal violation, we must face reality.

"Pornography, in all its forms, is one major cause of sex crimes, sexual aberrations and perversions.

"Is our society becoming so wicked that we are turning from virtue and integrity to immorality and degradation? Are we becoming morally bankrupt and letting our principles of conduct and decency deteriorate? Are we forsaking the simple teachings of right over wrong and good over bad?

"Let us look about us. In the publishing, theatrical and entertainment fields, are the good, enlightening and educational qualities of their products being overshadowed by too much emphasis on obscenity, vulgarity, incest and homosexuality?

"Many people believe this to be true. But the legitimate productions of these media are rather mild when compared with the 'hard core' pornography flooding the country in the forms of film, 'playing' cards, 'comic' books, paperbacks and pictures.

"Such filth in the hands of young people and curious adolescents does untold damage and leads to disastrous consequences.

"Police officials who have discussed this critical problem with me unequivocally state that lewd and obscene material plays a motivating role in sexual violence."

As is pointed out by this great advocate of law and order, "Pornography in all its forms, is one major cause of sex crimes."

We have pornographic films, pornographic advertising, pornographic magazines, books and posters, and shops which specialize in these things. Public newsstands are full of it.

Styles, both of men and women, have become largely pornographic. Tight, revealing clothing is as disgusting on men as it is on women. Shorter and shorter skirts are pornographic in the extreme.

All have their effect in boosting the sex crime now engulfing our nation and the world. And these are given further impetus by the demoralizing effect of liquor, now so freely and easily made available.

In some of the best residential areas of our cities, people are frightened to walk alone at night and particularly are girls and women not safe. Why? Who are the attackers? The sex deviates!

And why are there so many sex deviates?

Because perversion is made POPULAR by what we read and see and buy.

Every right-thinking parent wants his child to grow up in purity.

Then why do parents fail to take steps to further protect them?

It is all well and good for parents to talk and protest among themselves. BUT TO PROTECT OUR YOUTH WILL REQUIRE MORE THAN TALK.

We must use the available laws to fight pornography.

If laws are not adequate, then we must move to the legislature and demand sterner laws.

If courts do not cooperate in curbing this evil, then let us elect new judges.

If stores insist on selling smut, let the right-thinking populace wait upon the operators and demand a change. It is business they're working for, and they should know that decent people are still in the majority. The sad thing is that we are not as vocal as we should be.

Churches, schools, PTA organizations, all wholesome groups should band together to fight this menace.

If there ever was an ecumenical movement that deserves widespread support, it is the battle for decency. Surely all right-thinking people can unite on this point and FIGHT SMUT.

New Rules On Movies

THE MOTION PICTURE Association of America announces that it has a deep "concern for children."

This concern is seen in recent rulings by this organization to classify movies so that little children will be kept from vicious and licentious types if their parents will watch for the designations being provided by the manufacturers.

For some time there has been a wide demand that the United States government put an official brand on bad movies and indicate which pictures are safe for children.

The movie association did not relish such a step by the government, and so now has made its own listings as follows:

The letter "G" will indicate that a movie is fit to be seen by "general audiences."

The letter "M" will indicate movies which may be seen safely by mature audiences only.

The letter "R" will indicate showings for "restricted audiences," and the letter "X" will be the brand by which all may know that a picture is for adult audiences only.

One of the many difficult things about this listing is that children of 16 and over are rated as adults.

That means that 16-year-olds — just in the bloom of emerging sex emotions — will be allowed to see filthy sex films which will excite them to all sorts of deviations, from silent acts in the rear seats of automobiles or in motel rooms to open attacks on women and girls on the dark streets of almost every city in this land.

On this point it is of more than ordinary interest to note that a recent Gallup poll shows that 35 per cent of the white population and 40 per cent of the black population of America are afraid to venture out on the streets of their own home towns at night.

Fifty per cent of all the women in America are shown to be frightened to go out alone at night, in their own neighborhoods.

Most of these night attacks on women are sex attacks. They are made by perverts who even kill for sex gratification. And now the movies are producing "adult only" films to which they admit 16-year-old boys and girls, thus stimulating the very passions which can make perverts of them.

It is noted from the listing made by the Motion Picture Association that three out of the four classifications are intended to exclude children. Do they not see that so far as decent families are concerned, this action will keep families or unaccompanied children away from three-fourths or more of the films? Haven't children and families in the past been the best customers of movie houses?

Instead of stressing the "concern" these movie people have over children not seeing the filthy pictures, they should begin to make clean pictures which will be enjoyed by entire families — on a regular basis.

Why must the movie industry aid and abet the sex revolution which has swept this and other countries, and brought with it an epidemic of venereal diseases?

Motion pictures are among the strongest and best teaching tools known to education today. But why should they be debauched?

The volume of mail which comes to the editor's office protesting sex education in the schools is growing tremendously. Sex education in the schools also includes movies, some showing the most intimate of sex acts. They seldom provide the atmosphere of virtue in which the teaching of this delicate subject should be accomplished.

Now the commercial movie industry joins the schools in displaying sex in a manner which can only add to the promiscuities of the present day and to the revulsion felt by every decent parent.

Isn't it time for all right-thinking people to do something about the matter — both as to sex education in school and the additional "sex education" provided on the commercial screens?

In But Not Of The World

CHRISTIANITY IN EUROPE has all the symptoms of a dying religion, and Europe is showing the results in shocking respect.

More people drink and smoke there than ever before.

There are more disrupted marriages than ever before.

Fewer people attend church services than ever before.

There are more illegitimate children than ever before.

There is more promiscuity than ever before.

And there is more social disease than ever before.

Sane people, looking at the facts, can hardly understand how Europe would give up the uplifting and elevating life of a true Christian for the filth of the present day. Truly one may ask, "What will a man give in exchange for his soul?"

Two recent reports from Europe point up the ravages of sex looseness which exists there.

The British Council of Churches, after a two-year study on "sex and morality," refused recently to condemn pre-marital relationships.

Sweden, after ten years of frank sex education in schools, is now beginning to count the cost in terms of greatly increased venereal disease, more illegitimate births, and a realization that 80 per cent of their young people indulge in illicit relationships.

In Britain it is understandable that churchmen of various denominations would now take the position indicated, for many of them, even from the pulpit, have long since let down the bars on Christian morality. High government officials have done likewise. Homosexuality and prostitution even of 16-year-olds are legalized. With this attitude on the part of their leaders, can the people be expected to live clean moral lives?

In Sweden sex looseness has become the way of life. After ten years of teaching sex in school the Swedes now find that such instruction has greatly increased promiscuity, boosted venereal disease beyond anything they are willing to admit, and brought into the world thousands of illegitimate children. Most high school students there regard premarital relations as both natural and acceptable, an attitude stimulated by sex education in the public schools.

The public instruction on sex now given there includes lessons on how to use contraceptives. Youngsters are taught about abortion and sterilization also.

Sex instruction begins in the first grade, and continues through high school, intimate details being openly discussed in mixed classes. Contraceptives are available in vending machines, and everyone is invited to use them.

The Swedes thought that the use of these devices would protect them from venereal disease, but they are now shocked into a realization that there is no such protection, and that the incidence of the disease is skyrocketing in proportion to the increasing immorality of the country. Education does not influence the V.D. rate, which increases with exposure.

America has its share of this sort of thing, as do all other countries. The let-down in morals is not confined to Britain or Sweden. It is world-wide.

But as immorality is world-wide, so also is the decline in obedience to the Gospel of Christ. They go hand in hand.

Christ teaches righteousness and chastity. Because the world no longer desires the clean life, it begins to reject Christianity. So in the hearts of the masses of many countries, Christianity dies. When people no longer uphold Christian ideals, they are no longer Christian. In America both spirituality and morality are probably higher than in any other part of the world. For this we are thankful.

The scriptures indicate that in the latter days there will be a vast separation of the righteous from the wicked. That day will come. But in the meantime, the righteous must live among the wicked, in the world literally, yet they must never partake of her sins so that they will not receive of the plagues of V.D. and other diseases.

At least one group of people in the world is committed to a preservation of true Christianity — the Latter-day Saints.

The Gospel has been restored to them, and with it the scriptural law of virtue. Chastity is as much a part of the restoration of the Gospel as baptism or the resurrection. Without it there is no Christianity.

Latter-day Saints are under covenant to be true to the name of Christ. That requires devotion to His laws and commandments, among the most important of which is chastity.

Latter-day Saints must ever remember that it is better to die protecting virtue than to live an unclean life. Virtue is more important than life.

We are to emulate the example of Christ and become like Him. That is impossible without virtue.

In this Church young and old alike must preserve modesty as a safeguard to morality, and cling to Christ-like virtue as fundamental to our faith. This allows for no extreme styles inviting immorality, no petting, and no unchastity in the slightest degree.

Latter-day Saints must be clean, for they bear the vessels of the Lord.

Black, White, Or Gray?

PRESIDENT GEORGE ALBERT SMITH taught us to "stay on the Lord's side of the line."

Which line? That which is drawn between good and evil, between obedience and its opposite.

But is this a sharp line of cleavage, or is it indistinct, providing a "gray area" in which we may cross partly over, and still keep one foot on the Lord's side?

Does it allow us in this way to serve two contrary masters in an effort to get gain from both?

With the Lord there are no "gray areas." We are for Him or we are not. He asks us to serve Him with ALL our hearts, might and minds, and no one can give his all and still hold something back.

But many nevertheless try to create "gray areas" to justify their compromises. This they do in many ways.

Some drive a "bargain" to its legal limits, ignoring fairness in the transaction. Mercy and regard for the rights of others are not always considered a part of business.

But can business be divorced from Christian principles? Where is there greater need for the Golden Rule, for fairness, honesty and justice?

And what of our other standards? Is there a "gray area," for example, in our attitude toward the Word of

Wisdom? How far can we go toward the ways of the world and still claim to keep the law?

Suppose a man has many dealings with those not of our faith. How strict should he be with himself?

If he entertains in his home, should he provide them with all they are accustomed to in theirs?

If they are drinking people, should the Latter-day Saint host serve liquor to avoid depriving them of their accustomed "pleasures"?

Should he have cigarettes available in convenient places when they visit in his home?

Does he feel that these things are essential to good relationships with his non-member associates? Can true friendship be bought with a cocktail?

Other questions arise also:

Should a Latter-day Saint allow smoking in his home in any case, even by his invited guests?

Should he allow drinking in his home on the part of anyone?

Should he ever have liquor or tobacco in his possession, in or out of the home?

Many members of the Church hold high positions in places of state and national prominence, and in business and educational circles. They are known as Latter-day Saints by their friends, who also know the position of the Church on these matters.

Hundreds of such Latter-day Saints testify that their non-member friends EXPECT them to maintain Church standards and would be disappointed if they did not do so.

No guest would give affront to his host by smoking or drinking in his home when knowing the attitude of the family on the subject.

The average guest actually loses some respect for a host who lowers the bars for the sake of expediency.

Let not the host deceive himself on this point. The guests know quite well that serving liquor and tobacco is an expediency to gain some personal advantage with them, and that it is a compromise of standards on the part of the LDS host.

It is not enough for the host himself to abstain from smoking or drinking. His home — his hospitality — must reflect his personal standards, and every guest will respect him for it.

And what of the moral law? Does God allow any "gray areas" there? Can we be just a little unchaste and still please Him who said He cannot look upon sin with the least degree of allowance?

Is it not the same with filthy books and magazines? Their presence in our homes gives support to the adversary.

It is so in all we do. We must serve God with our whole heart, remembering that He allows for no "gray areas" where we may compromise with sin.

Keeping Our Standards

TWO YOUNG LADIES, one in high school and the other a freshman in college, wrote to President McKay a short time ago pledging their support to the standards of the Church.

Many such letters are written indicating the conversion of the youth of the Church to the righteous principles taught in the Gospel.

But this letter, signed by the two girls, was so touching, that the editors of the *Church News* published it in part. Said the letter:

"We're writing concerning an article we read in *Time* magazine which spoke of our Church lowering its standards to meet the demands of a changing society.

"We feel that our opinions represent the true members of the Church when we say we don't want the standards to be altered to conform with the 'Great Society.' The standards we realize are strict, but we are more than willing to abide by them, because they were commanded by God, not men.

"They cannot be altered by anyone except God. We know it is right to obey God's commandments. Obeying the commandments sets us apart from a world of unbelievers, showing that we are on God's side.

"Obedience makes us individual beings because we do not conform to the whims of the crowd. Obedience makes us happy. And lastly, the standards of the Church and obedience to them gives fulfillment and strength we know the world cannot supply.

"We are anxiously awaiting the time when we can enter the temple and receive our blessings and become one with those fortunate ones who have already partaken of them, the people we so greatly admire.

"When we see these people living the standards and striving to live righteously, we are determined to reach our goal — temple marriage.

"The Word of Wisdom is another point of controversy, but is a standard well worth living. Our bodies are our temples and we believe in keeping them clean and holy and pure.

"We refute any suggestion of change in God's marvelous laws for our benefit. We insist that the standards are not too difficult to be lived.

"We accept the responsibility of the straight and narrow way which will lead us to celestial glory.

"We acknowledge this challenge and extend it to the youth of our generation and those who follow.

"The way will never be easy, but we will never alter our course.

"You surely receive countless letters such as this one, but we wanted you, our Beloved Prophet and Leader, to know of our support. With ever increasing love and faith we terminate this letter."

(Signed by the two girls.)

Shall the youth of Zion falter?

Not while they retain this spirit. And the spirit of these two girls is reflected in the hundreds of thousands of other faithful youth who love the standards of the Church, and glory in observing them.

Those who suppose that the Church will change its fundamental doctrines to meet the exigencies of the times do not understand the Latter-day Saints.

A people who have been willing to give up homes, employment, and even loved ones, to preserve their faith, will not yield to the pressures of the day.

The youth of today are just as deeply converted as were those of the 1840s. Anyone attending a youth testimony meeting will discover this. Anyone living month in and month out with groups of full-time missionaries would discover this great fact very quickly.

The youth of Zion are faithful, and whereas there are some who drift away, much to our regret, the great masses continue to sing: "Shall the Youth of Zion Falter?" and reply with a positive "No!"

A Teenage World

ON ALL SIDES we hear adults deploring the activities of teenagers. They blame youth for the increase in crime, for our widespread immorality, and call them a rebellious generation. But can they do so rightly?

It is admitted that arrests of youths under 18 for serious offenses have increased 54 per cent in seven years, and 19 per cent for children from 10 to 17.

But arrests of persons under 18 made up only 23 per cent of the total police arrests in 1966. And even though this figure seems high — and is much too high, we all admit — we may be reassured to know that only 5 per cent of the total youth population of the country came before the courts for serious criminal acts.

Compare that 5 per cent with the millions of youths who are useful citizens, active church workers, Boy Scouts and participants in a host of other wholesome activities.

The fact is that 95 per cent of our young people do not get involved in serious trouble. Then why should the finger of blame be pointed so persistently at teenagers as a class?

Teenagers live in a world made by adults, and their standards reflect those of their elders. They can hardly be blamed for the sin in the world, for most of it is not of their making.

The adults, not the youth, set the pattern of major crime in America — 77 per cent of it.

It is the adults who publish pornographic books and magazines, not the youth.

The sensual and debasing movies are not the work of teenagers either, nor is the production, nor the acting, nor the distribution.

Can the youth be blamed for unwholesome radio and TV programs, or the suggestive Broadway plays that tour the nation?

Are they responsible for the shutting down of empty churches, or the denial of Christ by clergymen who claim that God is dead?

Who operate the houses of ill fame? Not the teenagers.

Who "rig" the elections, make the election "payoffs" and bribe receptive police officers? Not the teenagers.

And who are they who devise sports briberies, and persuade youngsters on the team to throw a game for a certain consideration?

Who defraud the governments in their tax returns? Who are the embezzlers, the bank robbers and the payroll snatchers?

What age group diverts government funds to personal use? Who robs the mails? Who are convicted of price fixing?

Who foment strikes and riots? Who are the anarchists and arsonists?

Who are the heaviest drinkers and consume most of the alcoholic beverages? Who bring liquor into the home for family consumption? Who spend their incomes at the gambling tables? Who fight the effort to protect the public from tobacco cancer and other smoking-induced ills? Who form the tobacco lobby in Washington?

Who are responsible for our record divorce rate, our abandoned families and the worst delinquency examples?

None of this can be laid at the door of our teenagers.

But on the other hand, who are the best church-goers in America? The teenagers.

Who are setting new and unheard of records in scholarship? The teenagers.

Who are filling most missions for our Church? And who are fighting the battles in Vietnam?

Before we lay too much stress on the downward trend of 5 per cent of the teenagers, let us pay some heed to the adults who lead them astray.

Most teens are good, honorable, forthright young people. In our Church it is the teenagers who make the best activity records. The teen attendance at sacrament meeting, for example, virtually doubles that of adults in many of our stakes.

It is the teen group that bears some of the most moving testimonies in fast meetings. It is our teenagers who carry an MIA program that has become the admiration of skilled observers the world over.

Our teens have one of the best behavior records to be found in any of the colleges anywhere.

The beatnik is absent from BYU and Ricks, nor are they enrolled among thousands of young people in seminary and institute classes.

Would adults leave their beds at 5 and 6 a.m., as many of our seminary students do, to attend weekday religious education classes five days a week?

The rising generation will be a great one if the adults do not spoil it. Given a fair opportunty, it will surpass the fondest hopes of its predecessors.

The great statesmen of tomorrow will come from the present generation of teenagers, as will the greatest scientists and educators.

And in the Church, the prophets of the years to come are already in training in our priesthood and auxiliary organizations as the teenagers of today.

"Familiar With Her Face..."

THERE IS A philosophical truth which needs constant re-emphasis:

"Vice is a monster of so frightful mien
As to be hated needs but to be seen,
Yet seen too oft — familiar with her face —
We first endure, then pity, then embrace."

—Alexander Pope

This is called to mind particularly as we read in current news dispatches suggestions in a recent Federal Government report, that the way to conquer alcoholism is to drink more liquor.

But just as astonishing is the further report that the National Council of Churches endorses the recommendation.

Some of the suggestions made by Uncle Sam's "experts" on alcoholism are:

Lower the drinking age to 18.

Permit colleges to serve alcoholic beverages in school cafeterias.

Publish advertisements showing alcohol being consumed by the entire family, including children.

Make liquor available to young people in church socials.

And increase drinking in the home and elsewhere as a means of replacing bars.

It is reported that it cost the American taxpayers a million dollars for this committee to produce these suggestions!!!

In another report a comparison was made between the use of liquor and tobacco with some claiming that alcohol is not as harmful as tobacco, and therefore should be made more a part of modern social graces.

However, medical officials show that alcohol is quite as injurious to health as is smoking, to say nothing of its moral hazards.

One of the most common and dangerous effects of drinking is contraction of cirrhosis of the liver, from which many people die each year. It is true that tobacco contributes to this disease, but not as much as liquor.

Alcohol is now found to be closely related to tuberculosis. Recent evidence has suggested that there may be a closer association with alcoholic consumption than with cigarette smoking in cases of this disease.

Cancer is the great plague of tobacco users, but it is also becoming one of the lethal enemies of alcohol users. Strangely enough, it is said that cancer of the mouth is on the rise among liquor drinkers. Although the facts are not fully known as to the cause, it is noted that there is a definite relationship between liquor and tobacco in causing this particular disease.

Mental disturbances are many among liquor drinkers. So are ulcers of the digestive tract, in some cases developing into cancer. Diseases of the nervous system are related to both liquor and tobacco.

We might go on. The fact is that both alcohol and tobacco are very dangerous to health.

But why do Uncle Sam's "experts" say that the cure for the ills of drinking is to drink more? Why don't they also say that the cure for health hazards in tobacco is to smoke more? The logic would apply equally well.

To bring more liquor into the home means more family drinking. Most young people who drink and smoke admit they started both habits in the home. Who can tell which of our youth will become alcoholics?

To bring liquor into religious gatherings is to defy the Providence who, throughout the Bible, condemns drunkenness.

To make drinking more general will add immeasurably to the death toll on highways, where it is being proven day by day that drinking causes more traffic fatalities than does any other one thing.

Vice really is a monster of hideous mien. Drinking, with all its ills — from broken homes to death from cancer — is just as hideous.

Can drinkers be so enamored of their liquor that they ignore these proven results?

Are they so "familiar with her face" that they suppose death and illness, divorce and debt — so intimately associated with drinking — are but a part of our way of life to be accepted without further investigation?

How much more beneficially could we have spent that million dollars in proper education against this vice, than to give it our complete approval and acceptance!

Spokane's Tobacco Experiment

FOR SIX YEARS the city schools of Spokane have carried on an experiment with tobacco.

Elementary and high school students during that period have been given the facts about the dangers involved in smoking. A sampling of high school seniors recently showed that only 14 per cent smoke at least one cigarette a day, compared to 29 per cent when the experiment began.

Of 205 seniors sampled this year, only six said they would advise a younger brother or sister to smoke, and one of them admitted "Yes, cuz I hate her."

Ninety-six per cent of the students who took the course offered in Spokane schools ended up with a negative attitude toward smoking. Some of their comments were:

"Smoking is for the birds."

"It's like selling your soul. Nothing is gained, all is lost."

"A girl who smokes looks like a tramp."

But one of the striking comments came in regard to adults — parents, public officials and school teachers in particular: "I'm sick and tired of adults worrying about teenagers smoking when they do it themselves."

This spring the Surgeon General of the United States announced that a million Americans a year are giving up smoking, but that in the first four months of this year 18,000 Americans died of lung cancer.

A nationwide survey recently asked smokers in every state the question: Do you want your children to smoke?

Eighty per cent replied stoutly with a positive "No!"

But even though thinking this way, millions of parents continue the habit. The report indicated that when smoking is a part of the normal, acceptable family practice, it becomes a natural part of growing up for a child to begin smoking at an early age.

About half the nation's teenagers are regular smokers by the time they are 18. The American Cancer Society points out that at this rate a million of the children now in school in the United States will die of lung cancer before they are 70, and many times that number will die of or be disabled by coronary heart disease, emphysema and circulatory diseases.

It is estimated that every day in this country about 4,000 children try their first cigarette.

The U.S. Surgeon General says that each year in America smoking causes:

Between 125,000 and 300,000 premature deaths.

300,000 coronary attacks.

2,000,000 cases of chronic bronchitis or emphysema.

2,000,000 cases of sinusitis.

1,000,000 cases of peptic ulcers.

Commenting on the attitude of parents, Dr. Harold S. Diehl, deputy executive vice president of the American Cancer Society in charge of research and medical affairs, says:

"Parents can help their youngsters avoid the cigarette habit before they are trapped by it. First, teach your children all the facts about the dangers of smoking. Second, set a good example for them. The opportunity is yours. You can protect your health and help your children act intelligently to protect theirs."

Serious as are the health factors in smoking, for Latter-day Saints there is an ever greater hazard. It is the loss of spirituality.

For us it is more than a health measure to avoid the use of tobacco — it is a matter of obedience to the Lord.

God has commanded the Latter-day Saints to avoid tobacco. It is His will and His word to us.

Whenever we resist the Lord, we lose a certain degree of spirituality.

But when we both resist Him, and at the same time fill our bodies with uncleanness, we place a double handicap upon ourselves. The Spirit of God will not dwell in unclean tabernacles.

Both obedience and cleanliness are requisite to our salvation.

"No Thank You, I Don't--"

TAKING A STAND becomes increasingly important to the Latter-day Saints.

But it must be a firm stand — for the right! In some instances it must even be a fighting stand where one must abandon old associates and find new ones having tastes and standards like our own. And there still are many of them, thank heaven!

Conditions are reaching a point where we must stand by our convictions and our religious teachings as a matter of self-defense if for no other reason. It is becoming almost a necessity for survival in health and peace.

Note a few cases in point.

Take the use of alcohol as an example. So-called social drinking is fast becoming almost universal. The liquor manufacturers have set an immediate goal to make at least three-fourths of the population consumers of their product.

In some circles we are not "one of the crowd" if we don't drink. So what do we do, surrender or find a different crowd?

Consider smoking. Must we smoke as the price of popularity? Or is it better to drop the smoking crowd?

Will smoking ultimately help you or hurt you? What does liquor do — for you or to you?

And morals, what of them? Is the so-called thrill worth the devastating price it exacts?

We have many boys in Vietnam. They have to take a stand also.

Clayton Fritchey's "State of Affairs" syndicated column says there are 4,000 "bar-fly" girls in Saigon alone and that at night a decent man must actually elbow his way through the gauntlet of sex solicitors, pornographers, night club outriders, and their ilk.

He says that venereal disease is the number one ailment of U.S. troops in Vietnam and that statistics of a year ago revealed that nearly one in every five servicemen contracted V.D.

Think of the effect on the individual soldiers! Think of the possible spread of the disease when those men return home!

The price is more than any nation can afford.

Our LDS fighting men in the war zone are taking their stand against this plague. They have organized themselves into scores of religious groups where spirituality is the key to purity. They are taking their stand both for cleanliness and for God. Can we do less?

And think of the liquor and tobacco toll here among us!

How do liquor and tobacco affect us?

Every doctor knows they destroy health and every promiscuous person knows they abet unchastity.

But they destroy spirituality too, and spirituality is our strongest defense against these plagues.

To surrender to worldliness is to invite disaster for ourselves and heartbreak for our families.

We often speak of the pestilences to come as part of the latter-day tribulations. But the diseases which come are those we bring upon ourselves.

The V.D. pestilence is already a vast world-wide problem. Nothing yet has stopped it. It is spreading like a subtle but deadly ground fire which no amount of wonder drugs can halt.

One doctor writes: "The medical profession, confronted with this sexual revolution, can only wash its hands and call itself an innocent bystander of our times."

The plague of alcoholism is but another self-induced pestilence of our times and with it the entire gamut of diseases related to it.

And likewise tobacco. It, too, is now found to be related to fatal diseases ranging all the way from heart trouble to cancer and showing itself increasingly in heart trouble, which is our number one killer. How much of this is self-induced?

Can we blame God for these modern pestilences as we bring them upon ourselves by our own foolhardy indulgence?

The scriptures say that the saints will be spared in these days of tribulation, but they will be saved only as they refuse to partake of the indulgences which create these plagues.

It is truly a matter of survival — physical, mental and spiritual.

If we would be free of them, we can follow but one path and that is the straight and narrow way which God defines.

"This Will Kill You"

THE NATIONAL TUBERCULOSIS Society is passing out posters showing a cigarette-smoking woman. The caption under it says:

"My dear, this'll kill you."

It is part of a new national drive against the use of tobacco. The momentum is growing so fast that the cigarette manufacturers are more worried than they have been since the Surgeon General's report on the dangers of smoking.

As the *Wall Street Journal* explains:

"To hear the tobacco companies tell it, everyone is out to get them. 'Tobacco critics are at work across the land,' says Joseph H. Cullman III, president of Phillip Morris Inc. Says Edwin J. Finch, president of Brown & Williamson Tobacco Corp.: 'The tobacco industry is under attack by powerful enemies.' Adds Michael Harris, president of Ligget & Myers Tobacco Co., 'Antitobacco activity continues to threaten us.'

" 'We are all part of a beleaguered force that is being attacked on one hand by tobacco-and-health charges and countercharges and on the other hand by antitobacco zealots,' says Fred S. Royster of Henderson, N. C., managing director of the Bright Belt Warehouse Association and president of the Tobacco Tax Council, a trade group.

"Things could be worse. In 1964, the year of the report to the Surgeon General linking cigarette smoking with health hazards, cigarette shipments fell 2.4 per cent; in 1965 they rose 2.8 per cent; in the first 10 months of 1966, they rose 2.5 per cent. Domestic consumption in 1966 was a record, the Agriculture Department estimates, though per-capita use was below the record of 1963.

"What's more, the U. S. tobacco industry, whose annual sales are more than $5 billion, spends $300 million a year to advertise. Its opponents have a total cash budget of less than $3 million a year.

"Why, then, is the tobacco Goliath so concerned about the anti-tobacco David?

"There already are indications, in fact, that more of the nation's young people are scorning cigarettes. Only 7 per cent of this year's freshman class at Princeton University said they smoke cigarettes, the lowest percentage since the school started keeping track in 1948. At Kelvyn Park High School in Chicago, more than 1,000 students have voluntarily pledged either to quit or never to start smoking.

"Evidence of the anti-smoking campaign is everywhere. In Maine, 30 large billboards in major cities carry a blunt message from the state's health department: 'Cigarette smoking is bad for your health.' On the Merritt Parkway in Connecticut signs on the median ask, 'Are you dying for a smoke?' Some 800 radio stations now run free anti-cigarette messages provided by the Government.

"The Federal Government has allotted $2.8 million this fiscal year for the Public Health Service to use in anti-smoking campaigns. Of this, $200,000 is being used in the Syracuse and San Diego areas for 'community laboratories' aimed at changing attitudes toward smoking."

The UPI recently reported:

"The California Medical Association has asked all physicians to quit smoking and urged the doctors to advise their patients against cigarette smoking.

" 'Surveys of physicians indicated that the majority accept the scientific evidence as a guide for personal behavior, and as a basis for giving advice to patients,' the council said. 'Physicians have stopped or changed their smoking habits more than any other group.' "

The American Medical Association's *AMA News* reported:

"Smoking Warning: The National Advisory Cancer Council blamed cigarette smoking for an 'enormous man-made epidemic of lung cancer.' It is estimated that 42,000 men and 8,000 women will have died during 1966 from lung cancer."

In England smoking has developed into a hot issue in Parliament. Health Minister Kenneth Robinson is planning curbs on smoking in all public places. He told the House of Commons that the lung cancer "epidemic" is now out of control. Nearly 200 British people die of lung cancer every day.

In the past the public has been slow to accept scientific findings about tobacco. But it is now being aroused, and every day more and more see that they may be "dying for a cigarette."

We Do Not Stand Alone!

MANY PEOPLE ARE ashamed of their religion, and many compromise their beliefs because they are afraid of the criticism of the world.

There are some Latter-day Saints in this category, particularly with respect to the Word of Wisdom.

Some actually feel that we are peculiar and alone in our position on liquor, tobacco, and tea and coffee. How mistaken they are!

The *New York Times* recently reported a convention of the Seventh Day Adventists. This denomination has a total membership of 1,600,000, of whom 380,000 are in the United States.

This group has not always been known as Seventh Day Adventists. It was formed prior to 1844 as an organization awaiting the second coming of Christ, which they expected on October 22 of that year.

When the expectation failed to materialize, a reorganization took place and in 1863 the presently known denomination took form.

One of the outstanding doctrines of this denomination, which does much good in the field of health, particularly with its hospitals and widely taught doctrines on foods, is its position on tea, coffee, liquor and tobacco, all of which are banned.

The Adventists regard the human body as the temple of the Holy Spirit and place great emphasis upon the relationship between the spiritual and one's mental and physical health.

It sponsors courses for non-Adventists who want to give up smoking and drinking and is currently concluding a 16-week weight-reducing course.

Its present plans call for 10,000 five-day anti-smoking courses in 50 countries in the next four years, and the launching of a similar effort to combat alcoholism.

It is of interest to note that the corn flake king, John Harvey Kellogg, a surgeon and dietician, became superintendent of that church's sanitarium at Battle Creek, Michigan, in the 1870s and invented more than one hundred nut and cereal products, to promote health.

But not only are the Adventists teaching abstinence from these harmful things, other churches are doing so also.

The Christian Science religion is strongly opposed to stimulants and narcotics, and has made a significant contribution to general education regarding the harmful effects of tobacco and liquor in particular.

Other smaller denominations are taking a similar position. So are many of the clergy in the larger denominations, although there is no semblance of a universal doctrine on these points among them.

How much more influential would they be if all denominations were to fight alcohol and tobacco, exposing them for what they are!

Some of their leaders say that tobacco and alcohol may be harmful physically but they do not affect one's religion. The fact is that the Spirit of God does not dwell in unholy tabernacles, and without that Spirit there is little spirituality.

How much good influence can a Scout leader exert if he reeks of tobacco, or if his breath is befouled by the tell-tale stench of stale liquor?

How influential is a tippling clergyman? Or one who smokes or swears?

Can they make friends and influence people for good?

If they are the leaders of boys, will they not lead them into alcoholism, a little at a time, or into spiritual decline, as well as causing the health hazard that tobacco produces?

Latter-day Saints can well take heart from the fact that they are no longer alone in their fight against these evils. Other denominations are now following our lead. Science is moving in our direction. Educators interested in this cause are increasing in number. Abstaining doctors now are counted by the thousands.

We are NOT alone.

But adding these "reinforcements" will not assure victory. With us, it is a matter of conversion. Every member of the Church would do well to exert his full efforts to keep and teach the Word of Wisdom. It is not a fad, nor a man-made doctrine. It is REVELATION!

The Dog Experiment

ONE OF THE most interesting research studies made recently was that conducted by Dr. Oscar Auerbach, pathologist at the East Orange, N.J., Veterans Administration Hospital, pertaining to dogs and cigarettes.

As reported in a recent issue of *Time* magazine, Dr. Auerbach taught some beagles how to smoke. Beagles were chosen because their lung structure somewhat resembles that of human beings.

The doctor opened the throats of ten dogs with a tracheotomy, and after healing, connected them to a smoking machine. They were allowed to begin their experiment very gradually, but later worked up to 12 cigarettes a day which in the doctor's opinion was equivalent to heavy smoking in a human being.

At first the cigarettes made the dogs sick, as they do humans starting the habit, but later the animals seemed to develop a taste for tobacco.

As reported in *Time*, the first dog died on the 24th day of the experiment. A second died 205 days afterward, and three more died within 14 months.

Post-mortems were performed on all of the dogs that died, and in each instance "massive damage" was reported in their lungs. The lung tissue in the last two dogs to die was so completely destroyed that according to *Time* magazine the doctors had difficulty telling just what had happened.

In the other dogs the results resembled emphysema in man. It was explained that the experiment was not carried on long enough to tell whether or not any cancer would develop.

One part of the experiment, *Time* explains, was to perform tracheotomies on other beagles which were not subjected to the smoking machines. These non-smoking dogs were also examined after the same length of time, and were found to have perfectly healthy lungs.

Dr. Joseph G. Molner, writing a nationally syndicated health column carried in the *Deseret News,* explained that he has quit smoking because of the many health hazards in tobacco. Said he:

"In my case, I knew, as a physician, how much damage smoking can do. It doesn't take many cigarettes to establish the habit, and 20 or 30 or 40 years of smoking can do a lot of harm.

"We have very convincing statistics about the great increase in lung cancer among middle-aged people who have smoked for years, but that isn't necessarily the reason that is most impressive to physicians who know what ELSE smoking can do.

"Statistics are building up to show how much more heart trouble afflicts habitual smokers. Bronchiectasis, asthma, emphysema and other breathing difficulties are common and in time dangerous.

"I know one famous physician who gave up tobacco because he needed to get more sleep. Until he quit cigarettes he rarely slept a night through without waking up coughing.

"An even more famous surgeon who used to burn up four packs a day stopped because the nicotine was playing hob with the circulation in his legs, and a surgeon can't work unless his legs are steady for hours at a time."

Experiments will continue in this field. And with each new experiment will come further evidence of the divine inspiration which came to the Prophet Joseph Smith as revealed in the Word of Wisdom.

The Word of Wisdom is not only a guide to health. It is becoming much more than that. It is developing into one of the greatest of all testimonials that Joseph Smith was indeed a prophet of God, and that his work bears the stamp of both authenticity and divinity.

No uninspired man, more than a century ago, could have written into the Word of Wisdom what we read there today. No uninspired man could know that a century after Joseph Smith was in his grave, evidence would rise through scientific research to testify in unmistakable terms that "tobacco is not for the body, neither for the belly, and is not good for man."

But the same inspiration also said that neither strong nor hot drinks were good either, and as research upholds the inspiration of Joseph Smith in regard to tobacco, so it does likewise with respect to liquor, tea and coffee. The Word of Wisdom is TRUE.

Should Children Drink?

IF HIGHLY TRAINED doctors of medicine and psychiatry advocate liquor drinking by children as young as four years of age, will you believe them?

In the February, 1969, issue of *Today's Health,* published by the American Medical Association, there appears a panel discussion by three eminent scholars, two of them psychiatrists and one an internist, all of them experts in the field of narcotics and alcohol.

The subject of the discussion was: "Should children be taught to drink?"

Incredible as it is that such a subject would even be considered for discussion in a respected medical journal, it is more unbelievable that these highly schooled experts would agree among themselves that children should be "introduced" to alcohol at an early age, probably as young as four.

All three experts were opposed to alcoholism and appeared earnestly to seek a way to abolish it, but none even suggested abstention.

They regarded alcohol as an essential part of modern life, such as automobiles, for example, and felt that people — even youngsters — should learn to handle their alcohol as they learn to handle their cars.

To the question: "Should children be taught about drinking?" one of the psychiatrists answered: "Yes, if they intend to be drinkers during their lives." He went on:

"All our teaching about alcohol is fear-oriented, full of horror stories about the evils of drink. If we are ever going to prevent alcoholism as an emotional illness, we need to develop healthy attitudes in people, starting when they are young."

The doctors admitted that alcoholism is bad, and that most alcoholics had alcoholic parents; that most drinkers started drinking in their homes by the time they were 14, and that they learned to drink from their parents.

Their main criticism was that when parents drink they do not do it "as a ritual," making something "sacramental" out of it, adding that if the parents would drink "culturally" in the home and teach their little ones to do likewise, there would be fewer alcoholics.

One of them recommended that this "ritual" with the children begin at about four years of age with diluted wine, which could be given less and less dilution as the children grow up. If drinking was "ritualistic," with ceremony and "culture" at the dinner table, extremes would be avoided and thus there would be fewer drunkards, it was said.

It all seems so unbelievable! But there was one thing they said which was easily understood, and that was an admission by the psychiatrist for the New York State Narcotics Commission:

"I also want to say that it ought to be clear that we are speaking largely from hypothesis. This is an educated guess, a calculated reasoning by people in the field. But it's far from scientifically proved or really firm."

Thank heaven for that admission!

Of course it is not scientific! Of course it is purely guesswork! But why do men of this standing in scienti-

fic circles advise parents to teach their children to drink
— if only they do it culturally and with "ritual" — when
they admit there is no scientific basis for such advice?

They may talk about not liking the horror stories
accompanying reports on drinking, but those horror
stories cannot be brushed aside.

It is still a fact that of every 50 cars approaching
you on the highway, one is being driven by a person
who is drunk — not just drinking, but drunk.

It is still a fact, as pointed out by *U.S. News and
World Report,* that drunken drivers took 25,000 lives
last year alone, and that there were 800,000 crashes
due to alcohol in the nation last year.

It is also a fact that highway slaughter takes more
lives and causes more injuries than all our wars. Up to
1961 in America 1,375,000 persons were killed on highways, compared to 1,125,000 killed in all the wars in
which we have ever been involved. These same wars
listed 1,275,000 wounded, compared with 48,000,000
injured on the highways.

In Westchester County, New York, over an eight-
year period, 49 per cent of all drivers in fatal single-car
accidents were drunk, and an additional 24 per cent had
been drinking but not adjudged as drunk. In Montana
48 per cent of all drivers killed in auto accidents were
drunk. In Buffalo a check showed that 55 per cent of all
accidents involved liquor.

Shouldn't we have horror stories about liquor?

When will we accept God's word? Alcohol is not good
for man!

Should Children Drink? -- No. 2

REFERENCE HAS BEEN made to the theory propounded recently by three scholars that the way to eradicate alcoholism, which is now such a curse to mankind, is to teach children how to "handle their liquor" so that they will not carry drinking to an extreme when they grow up.

The fallacy of such a proposal of course is obvious.

But should children drink? The fact is that many of them do, shocking though it is.

Most drinking children acquire the habit in their own homes, being given liquor by their parents. Some observers actually have seen beer-drinking mothers help year-old babies sip from their mugs.

Drinking parents naturally and generally have drinking children. Most alcoholics have alcoholic parents. But most abstainers have abstaining children, and, strange as it may seem to the scholars, there are no alcoholics among them.

If the nation wants to know how to combat and eradicate alcoholism, it may find a simple answer in: "Don't drink."

Abstention can cure the alcohol plague of America. Abstention would protect the morals of youth, and cut down the automobile accidents by nearly 50 per cent. Abstention would save more than 25,000 lives on highways every year, and reduce automobile injuries by almost a half million.

If this or any other country is serious about abolishing alcoholism, they should consider abstention instead of suggesting that we teach youngsters how to drink "culturally" in the vain hope that it will protect them from over-indulgence.

Liquor and tobacco are recognized by medical authorities as disease-inducing commodities. The government has warned against both, but has hesitated to take serious statutory steps against them because both represent "big business."

Certain members of Congress are to be congratulated on their efforts to join the courageous FCC in a recommendation that tobacco advertising be banned from TV and radio. It has taken a long time — and many lives — to bring our lawmakers to this point. It is estimated that 50,000 people in the nation die of lung cancer alone each year.

But 25,000 died last year on our highways in 800,000 liquor-caused accidents.

If we are willing to take legal measures to reduce deaths from tobacco-induced cancer, why not take similar steps to halt liquor-induced deaths and injuries?

Much as the liquor proponents hate the word "prohibition," it is not unreasonable to suppose that some important restrictive measures will be taken in the future with respect both to liquor and tobacco.

After all, life must be regarded as worth more than business, and if any business is operating at the expense of thousands of lives each year, it should be dealt with.

We make a great deal of the water and air pollution problems and are quite willing to legislate against them.

But do they take more lives in proportion than do liquor-induced accidents and lung cancer?

Death-dealing commodities and practices should be placed in their proper perspective and dealt with accordingly.

How grateful the Latter-day Saints should be that more than a century ago the Lord gave to them sound guidance on the matter of narcotics and stimulants.

As a word of wisdom, adapted to the capacity of the weakest among us, He said:

"Inasmuch as any man drinketh wine or strong drink among you, behold it is not good." How plain is that statement!

"And, again, strong drinks are not for the belly." Can anyone misunderstand that language?

"And again, tobacco is not for the body, neither for the belly, and is not good for man." Research has proven this so completely that it is a wonder that anyone any longer uses the weed.

"And again, hot drinks are not for the body or belly." It is interesting that the new research which has concentrated so much on widely used stimulants now brands tea and coffee as enemies to health.

We are presumably a Christian nation. A Christian nation should believe in Christ.

The merciful God, who is interested in sparing His children from the ills of narcotic influences, has given us sound advice to abstain. Do we have the faith and good judgment to obey Him?

Get Really "Turned On"

SHAKESPEARE WROTE ABOUT "a rose by any other name." He knew that names are important, but not conclusive in identification.

People talk today about things that "turn you on." It may be an exciting type of music, or certain kinds of companionship, or even substances that take you on a "trip." Speaking in today's parlance they all "turn you on."

The immediate question that arises is: Turn you on to what?

Companionships can "turn you on," it is true, into either safe paths or dangerous ones, into a good life or its opposite. They become junction points having both right turns and wrong ones. It is admitted that they "turn you on," always toward your next step in life. But what kind of a step will it be?

Consider music of various kinds. Some will "turn you on" by stimulating you to exalting moments. The great classics do that. Oratorios, such as "The Messiah" by Handel, can lift one into ecstacies. Martial music can bolster our courage, and patriotic songs heighten our regard for our country. Symphonies and operas thrill us.

But, on the other hand, there is sensual music. It also "turns you on," but to degradation and filth. It stirs baser instincts and, when combined with suggestive bodily motions, can "turn you on" to adulterous relationships.

One of today's greatest "turner on-ers," as the youngsters put it, is the use of drugs. And what do they do, help you or hurt you?

They can send you insane! This they have done to thousands of young Americans.

In one state mental hospital, admissions of individuals for emotional problems resulting from the use of drugs has gone up in a ratio of one to 47 in a two-year period. Another large hospital reports that within a year there has been an increase of 400 per cent in the number of youngsters aged 18 to 20 admitted with serious mental problems resulting from the use of drugs.

Presumptions on the part of some young people, sometimes encouraged by certain ones who claim some medical knowledge, that marijuana is no more harmful than tobacco, are proving to be completely false.

Marijuana like tobacco is habit-forming, but it is also destructive of mental health, and can destroy the entire future of young people who indulge.

The more powerful drugs, beyond any question, are causing mental problems of such seriousness that some of the patients may never recover.

In one typical community, as reported by the Associated Press recently, where 3,000 babies are born annually, one in every five will require mental health service because of the stimulants taken by the mothers, and at least 240 of those 3,000 will become patients in mental hospitals. All because their mothers wanted something to "turn them on."

Is this the kind of "turning on" that Latter-day Saints want?

What is the principal objective of our lives, and how shall we plan for it? Is it a noble aim to drug one's self into a stupor, thus becoming irresponsible, weak, a prey to every predatory person?

Is a "trip" taken mentally by use of a drug so desirable that one would risk his sanity for the rest of his life to "enjoy" it? Is there anything desirable in hallucination anyway? Or is it the clear cool mind that assures success and true happiness?

And what can give us this clarity of mind?

Clean living. Good health. Spirituality, and freedom from stimulants of all kinds, including alcohol.

Inspiration from heaven is available to every one of us under proper conditions. The constant guidance of the Holy Spirit is promised to us if we live as we know we should.

Which is to be preferred — divine inspiration or hallucinations?

Which encourages success in school or at work — inspiration or a drug-induced stupor?

Which will help to preserve chastity — divine guidance or addiction to demoralizing narcotics?

Which will give us proper standing in the world — a clear mind or a clouded one?

So what is it that really "turns us on"? Only one thing: The Spirit of God, which comes to all who sincerely live the Gospel, and every faithful believer in Christ is entitled to its ministrations.

Handicap In Court

MUCH IS SAID these days about the diseases which follow in the wake of both smoking and drinking.

Recently *Listen* magazine, in an editorial by Francis A. Soper, its editor, pointed out the handicaps that face drinkers when they have accidents and have to go to court.

Mr. Soper wrote:

"No batter in the game of baseball would wish to step up to the plate with a strike automatically called against him before he starts.

"Yet that is comparable to what happens when a person takes a case involving his own use of alcohol into court and expects a jury to decide that case.

"It is generally assumed that evidence of consumption of alcohol by a party to a lawsuit will react to his disadvantage.

"The extent to which this is true is graphically illustrated in a series of reports drawn up by the Jury Verdict Research, Inc., of Cleveland, Ohio, for reference by insurance companies.

"In these reports it was found that when the plaintiff in a personal-injury case is alleged to have been drinking at the time of the occurrence it reduces his chances of winning his case by 44.5 per cent, a reduction of almost one half.

"The reductions from normal recovery rates within various liability situations were shown to be as follows: pedestrians struck by vehicles, 43 per cent; driver vs. driver cases, 52 per cent; drivers colliding with objects, 38 per cent; carrier accidents, 31 per cent; passenger cases, 66 per cent; occupier liability, 13 per cent; work injuries, 7 per cent.

"The allegation that the plaintiff had been drinking reduces the award he would otherwise expect to receive by an average of 25 per cent.

"If the plaintiff in a personal-injury case claims, with some substantiation, that the defendant had been drinking prior to the accident, it increases the plaintiff's chances of winning his case by 27 per cent, and reduces the defendant's chances of winning by 43 per cent.

"In other words, it can be said that either plaintiff or defendant, who is claimed to have been more or less under the influence of intoxicants at the time of an accident, stands a much smaller chance of winning his case than if no such allegation had been made.

"When both plaintiff and defendant in a personal-injury suit are claimed to have been drinking, it reduces the plaintiff's rate of recovery by 15 per cent. Conversely, the defendant wins 24 per cent more of these cases than those in which alcohol is not an issue.

"It is evident, then, that anyone involved with alcohol has much less chance in court to win verdicts and awards favorable to himself. A jury which finds alcohol to be an ingredient in any case is loathe to overlook its significance and immediately chalks up one strike against the batter!

"Why would anyone want to go up to bat with a strike already against him?"

In previous articles Mr. Soper has pointed out, as have many others, that not only do drinkers handicap themselves in court, but in every other way.

Drinking handicaps one in business, despite the custom of drinking cocktails as part of the process of "warming up" a business deal.

It handicaps a person in school.

It handicaps him in the home. Many divorces follow in the bitter wake of alcohol.

It corrupts morals, and lowers the bars of resistance to such a point that many indulgences occur that never would happen were the persons involved sober.

It boosts crime tremendously.

Is there one good thing that can be said about drinking?

It is one of the major threats to our happy existence today.

The drinker certainly "goes to bat" with at least one — and often two — strikes against him.

The Year's Understatement

From Williamstown, Massachusetts, comes a letter enclosing an editorial from the *North Adams Transcript,* entitled "Smoking is Dangerous."

Because of the interest in its subject matter, we reproduce below, with full credit to the *Transcript,* its editorial:

"Caution. Cigarette Smoking May Be Hazardous To Your Health."

This warning, contained in the tiniest of type on every cigarette package, may turn out to be the understatement of the century.

Actually, the warning was never strong enough. The government decreed that it must be printed on every package only after cigarette manufacturers had managed to defeat demands that much more positive and stringent warnings be included not only on every pack of cigarettes but in every advertisement for them.

And the case for a stronger warning — even for banning cigarettes entirely as a poisonous health hazard — was contained in the 1964 report of the U.S. Surgeon General on smoking.

Now comes a supplement to that report which strengthens and extends the original findings.

Among other things, the new report strongly indicates that smoking can cause many more ailments —

many of them often fatal ailments — than cancer, the
big villain of the original government report.

For example, take the new report's conclusions on
heart disease. Between the ages of 45 and 54, it was
found, male smokers of 10 or more cigarettes a day are
three times more likely to die and female smokers twice
as likely as persons who never smoked regularly. One
of the reasons for this, the researchers found, is that
nicotine increases the heart rate and output, resulting
in an increased demand for oxygen by the heart muscle.
At the same time the carbon monoxide in cigarette
smoke, competing with oxygen for passage through the
blood stream, causes a decrease in the oxygen available
to the heart at a time when the heart's need for it is
increased. Furthermore, smoking speeds up the forma-
tion of blood clots, which may result in coronary throm-
bosis.

In short, the report concludes, the evidence "strongly
suggests that cigarette smoking can cause death from
coronary heart disease."

When it is realized that heart disease is an even
bigger killer than lung cancer, the real significance of
this finding becomes obvious.

As for lung cancer itself, the new report states that
an eight-and-a-half year follow-up study of 290,000 veterans showed that persons aged 55 to 64 who smoked
two packs a day were 34 times more likely to die of lung
cancer than were non-smokers. The report also states
that smokers are four to five times more apt to die from
cancer of the esophagus and three to 19 times more apt
to incur cancer of the larynx than non-smokers.

In addition, a national health survey found that the
incidence of peptic ulcers was almost 100 per cent greater among male smokers and over 50 per cent greater
among female smokers than among non-smokers.

The report also cited an association between smoking and such diseases as stroke, aortic aneurism, emphysema, and cancer of the mouth, pharynx and bladder.

Obviously, if lung cancer, with its high death rate, did not already present enough hazard to justify the strongest possible efforts to discourage the use of cigarettes, these other diseases would.

It is too much to hope that warnings on packages and in advertisements will alone prevent people from smoking cigarettes — particularly people who are already "hooked" by the habit.

But warnings and greater education in the hazards of smoking may deter some young people from smoking so much that they get the habit.

And certainly, there is evidence enough now to justify rewriting the cigarette warning to read not that smoking "may be hazardous," but to state the truth in simple language:

"Warning: Cigarette Smoking Is Dangerous To Your Health and May Cause Death From Cancer Or Other Diseases."

Most Adults Don't Drink

A BRAND RATING Index, recently published in a medical journal, indicates that 5.9 per cent of the 117,000,000 adults in the United States drink 47.8 per cent of the hard liquor consumed in this country.

Twenty per cent of the adult population are reported to be total abstainers, with another 10 per cent drinking so infrequently that they can be classed as abstainers.

The report indicated another 30 per cent, totaling 35,000,000 people, spend less than $5 per year for liquor.

So about 60 per cent of the adult population adds very little to the liquor traffic.

But among the other 40 per cent there is a great deal of drinking, and at a high cost.

The report noted that most money "per drink" was spent by business executives, who averaged $2.90 per day for liquor, with the top figure reaching $7 per day, since this group uses the most costly brands.

Statistics indicate that most teenagers who drink learn to do so in their own homes, and that parents not only set them the example, but actually provide the liquor for them.

This trend is creating consternation among the organizations now fighting alcoholism, who see in it a rapidly growing threat to the younger generation who are turning more and more to think mistakenly that liquor is the door to social acceptance.

But the fact that 60 per cent of the population is virtually free from the use of liquor is most encouraging.

As many are now turning away from the use of tobacco for health reasons, so a good many are beginning to turn from liquor for the same reason.

However, the liquor interests are invading certain groups heretofore thought to be fairly safe from their allurements.

At a recent convocation of Methodists, a relaxing of the church tenets against the use of alcohol was attempted, but was battled vigorously by those who sought to hold the line which had made Methodists famous in their fight against drink.

A survey had shown that 61 per cent of Methodists above 15 years of age use liquor at some time. Advocates of relaxing the stand of that church against its use argued that "the policy of abstinence is producing hypocrisy and a loss of integrity in the corporate life of the church and in the lives of many ministers and laymen."

It had been recommended that the church do away with a pledge long held sacred among Methodists requiring clergymen to be complete abstainers, and that whether a layman drinks or not be left to the discretion of the individual.

These recommendations were fought vigorously and vehemently.

So far as Latter-day Saints are concerned, they can take but one position. If they believe in the revelations of the Lord to the Prophet Joseph Smith, they must be abstainers, and must do all within their power to teach their children to follow this example.

They must take a position against any movement which would relax the curbs on liquor, and must support public officials in enforcing the law.

To make liquor more readily available is to add to the number of alcoholics. Who can tell which of us will become an alcoholic? Whose home will be wrecked? Whose virtue will be lost?

The liquor question is a moral one. Liquor at no time has added to virtue, stability or good character. Always it has had the opposite effect.

This is not to say that everyone who uses it is a weak character, for that would be an unjust statement.

But it is true that liquor is an evil which is weakening the nation as a whole, adding to the crime rate, leading many into acts which they would never commit if they were sober, and which constantly tends to break down home life and family ties.

For us there can be only one position — control liquor and fight its demoralizing effects, even as we would fight any other evil.

Tobacco War Goes On

IT MAY TAKE another generation to wipe out smoking and its evils.

Our present generation forms the battle force which we hope will bring forth the necessary victory for the next one.

But the battle goes on, and furiously. Tobacco manufacturers of course are fighting to the death to protect their business, and we may expect them to continue to do so.

And yet, stronger forces in greater numbers are constantly arising to expose the tobacco habit for what it is — a deadly enemy of mankind.

In Albany, N.Y., Health Commissioner Hollis S. Ingraham of that state has called for a renewed "war" on cigarettes and asks that smoking be outlawed in all schools and public buildings in the state of New York. He classes smoking as "an epidemic of disease unique to the Twentieth Century."

"I can state unequivocally," he said, "that the cigarette is an agent of disease — cancer, heart and respiratory illness."

He called upon the state of New York to institute intensive instruction in all schools pertaining to the hazards of smoking, and urged the enlistment of all parent-teacher organizations in an anti-smoking crusade.

With financial assistance from the U.S. Public Health Service, the National Congress of Parents and Teachers has begun a campaign which they hope will develop "the first smokeless generation since man started putting shredded tobacco leaves into tubes of paper."

Over two and a half million families in 21 states joined the movement. According to H. Carl Smith, national project director, the program is moving forward with "unbelievable momentum." It will be taken into all 50 states within a year.

One of the sad comments arising out of this movement is that "emulation of adult behavior accounts for most of the smoking among children and youth."

Recently the magazine *Business Week* reported the first World Conference on Smoking and Health held in New York City, attended by 511 public health experts from all over the United States and 33 other countries.

All were reported to be eagerly seeking the latest reports linking tobacco to disease. All were anxious to launch crusades for "citizen action against cigarette smoking."

Dr. William H. Stewart, U.S. Surgeon General, recently issued a report entitled "The Health Consequences of Smoking" which is a companion to the 1964 report of the same federal office entitled "Smoking and Health."

The Surgeon General says "there is no longer any point of controversy among reasonable men" on the subject of tobacco and health.

Dr. Daniel Horn of the Public Health Service says that the cigarette habit "has suddenly turned into a monster, and we are hooked, both as individuals and as society."

Last September *Business Week* published several pages of suggestions under the heading "So You Want to Quit Smoking," together with a report on Senator

Robert Kennedy's attack upon the habit.

Other nations continue their work on the smoking evil also. Only recently the Italian government, which obtains 10 per cent of its annual revenue from the state tobacco monopoly, announced a nationwide campaign against smoking, as published in a recent issue of the *A.M.A. News* for the American Medical Association.

In England tobacco provides the government nearly three billion dollars in tax revenues every year, but even that country is taking further steps to curb smoking. To date it has done more officially than the United States in that direction.

No longer are there any doubts about the lethal effects of tobacco on health. The problem now is the smoking public.

The question arises: Why do people continue to smoke when the facts are so revealing and frightening?

And the answer? It may require a new generation to conquer the habit. The present one seems to prefer to run the risk, hoping that "it won't ever happen to me."

What Does God Think?

IN ALL THE debate over a new morality, use of intoxicating beverages, violence and crime, has anyone stopped to ask seriously what God thinks about these things? And would we accept His word if it were made known?

The tendency is to make up our minds on a basis of our own selfish purposes. As an editorial in a recent issue of *Parents'* magazine sadly said, "We are no longer willing to make arbitrary rules about what is good or bad, or right or wrong in behavior . . . we develop our styles of life according to individual judgment and decision. . . . The 'thou shalt not' approach does not convince the new generation."

Man is not all-sufficient. He does not know everything. He is not — even in this enlightened age — capable of making decisions on all things for the simple reason that, enlightened as he may be on some points, his mind is still darkened by both ignorance and prejudice on many others. Indeed, in spite of all our present knowledge, we still "see through a glass darkly," a glass made darker by our own selfishness and wilfulness.

When we say that we no longer can obey the "thou shalt nots" we in effect say we cannot accept Him who laid down those restrictions in the greatest code of law ever devised.

Setting aside the Author of the "thou shalt nots" of the Ten Commandments is to assume also that our human knowledge and judgment are superior to His. How modest we mortals are ! ! !

We are reminded of a comment on this subject made by Albert Einstein before his death. Writing in "The World as I See It," this mastermind said: "The harmony of natural law reveals an Intelligence of such superiority that compared with it, all the scientific thinking and acting of human beings is an utterly insignificant reflection."

And the magazine editor implies that we have outgrown all that! ! !

People who believe in God should be glad to accept His word on faith. God does not explain all He knows to finite human beings. Neither do the great scientists, for that matter. Don't we accept on faith the word of atomic researchers, of space men, and experts in any line? Then shall we not take on faith what God says about behavior?

The new morality is actually an invitation to free love. Editors, educators, lawmakers, and even some clergymen may approve and advocate it, but does that make it right? What does God say about sex freedom? What about His "thou shalt not" on this subject? Are we to set it aside because some supposedly "all-knowing" psychologist does so?

The same may be said about violence. In America we seem to condone violence until it strikes some great personality like Mr. Kennedy. But what does God say about violence — about murder? Are we to set that aside just because God — and not some magazine editor — said it?

There has been raging in Utah a controversy over liquor by the drink, and its value in attracting more business to the state. Has anyone ever thought to ask what God thinks about liquor and follow it? Is not a vote in favor of liquor a vote against His Word of Wisdom?

The fact of the matter is that man is not omniscient. Shocking as it may seem to some, he does not have all the wisdom. And a further sad fact is that the more man puts his trust in himself, the further he drifts from the God whom he professes to worship.

Generally man's judgment on behavior is based on his own likes and dislikes more than on what is basically right or wrong. Selfishness is at the heart of most behavioral problems.

Man so often resembles his own little children who won't eat this or that because they don't happen to like it, or who won't leave the water tap or the kitchen stove alone because they want them for playthings.

What parent would admit that a child's unwise whims should become the controlling factor in making important decisions?

Just as parents lay down rules of conduct for their little ones without entering into long and detailed explanations, so God has given us His "thou shalt nots" without necessarily giving chapter and verse as to His reasons.

Isn't it enough to know that He invites us to become like Him and that His laws are but guideposts to help us on our way? We can and must accept them on faith if for no other reason than just that God said so!

A Letter And A Message

THE FOLLOWING LETTER was recently received by the Church editor:

"I had an experience a few nights ago which I feel I should mention to you.

"We had spent the evening at the cabin of some friends in upper Ogden Canyon, and as we drove home we found it necessary to telephone back to our friends at their cabin.

"Accordingly we spent a half hour or so looking for a telephone. While I was making the call, an attractive young girl approached my wife sitting in our car in the parking lot, and asked if we would give her a ride to Ogden.

"It developed that she had been offended and frightened by her boy friend at a picnic ground lower down in the canyon. She left his car and walked alone up the dark canyon looking for a telephone to call some friends to come for her.

"Being unsuccessful, and becoming more and more afraid, in desperation she approached a total stranger, my wife, for help.

"In the course of her conversation she had said that she was afraid to call her parents as they would 'die' if they knew she was in this situation.

"She said, 'We are awfully religious; I don't suppose you are LDS, are you?'

"When my wife told her that I was a bishop, she exclaimed in relief: 'Oh, I did come to the right car, didn't I?'

"Two or three things impressed us about this experience:

"First, the long-shot coincidence of a bishop stopping at a public telephone booth around midnight in upper Ogden Canyon, and finding there a lovely LDS girl seeking help.

"Second, and more to the point, I was impressed by the fact that she was afraid to call her parents.

"Here was a girl of obvious courage, having dared to leave the car of her boy friend and walk up the dark canyon and approach a stranger for help, but yet without the courage to let her parents know of her danger and her need.

"It reminded me of how a friend some years ago told me that he had taken his daughters to one side and told them: 'Any time you need my help, wherever you are or under whatever conditions, all you need to do is call and I will come to you.'

"I have told my own daughter this, and the result has been that I have done a good deal of taxiing her and her friends around, but I have enjoyed every minute of it.

"I wonder if an effective editorial might be written urging parents to let their children know they love them and that they are ready to help under any conditions, and urging children to confide in their parents, and call on them whenever they may need help.

"Also, of course, young people should be cautioned to avoid getting into such situations in the first place."

This letter, telling of this experience firsthand, was far more effective than mere editorial comment. For this reason the letter is published.

Many young people are frightened of their parents, even though those parents may be good people, pious and religious like the parents of this girl.

But some parents are too stern. They fail to use the spirit of love and understanding in helping to shape the lives of their young people.

Iron rule does not make for trust and confidence. It can only develop fear in the minds of young people. And when a boy or girl is in difficulty, it is only natural for them to avoid the tongue-lashing they feel will almost certainly come from an overly stern parent, and for this reason they attempt to escape the best they can without letting the parents know of their problems.

Proper understanding and mutual love and trust between parents and children are vital to good family relationships. When parents fail to build this confidence in the minds of their children, they fail in a matter which far transcends the importance of an appearance of angelic piety.

A Bastion Of Salvation

"CRIMINALS ARE MADE — not born."

This was the declaration of J. Edgar Hoover, the great head of the FBI, in an address given in Chicago before a large convention of women.

"The blame for crime," he went on, "must be placed where it rightly belongs — upon the adult." Then he continued:

"A new sense of responsibility must be born in the home if we are to reverse the rising trend of youth toward lawlessness. Reasonable discipline, administered with consistency, is essential in developing a stable individual.

"This situation, in the final analysis, is not the failure of youth but the failure of adults. The fact remains that out of every 100 boys and girls in the 10-to-17 age group, 97 live law-abiding lives. There is nothing basically wrong with the youth of the land. Youth needs only to be guided along the proper path. A youth's intelligence must be anchored in morality to give him the ability to determine right from wrong, good from bad, and the true from the false. Given discipline, young people will learn self-discipline; given training, they will learn to live useful lives. The three out of each 100 who annually break the law have wandered into a morass of disbelief — where they have no faith, no belief in a Supreme Being, no respect for the rights of others, no belief in the dignity of man, and finally, no belief in themselves.

"There must be training for parenthood as well as a fixing of responsibility for the failure of parenthood. Too many parents allow their children to run free with no check on what they do, where or with whom they go. The result is a juvenile jungle.

"Too many homes breed juvenile delinquents through parental neglect. Too many children are left to shift for themselves — hungry, helpless, loveless.

"When parents are not sufficiently interested to know where their children are and what they are doing, the risk for their future is grave. It is the parents who should be brought before the bar of justice to account for their stewardship when their children go astray. The parents are responsible to a great extent for the sins of their children. The parents should be held morally, legally, and financially responsible.

"I have studied the case histories of thousands of criminals. In almost every case, the failure to develop character is directly attributable to lack of proper influence and guidance in the home. Unfortunately, the home no longer provides the inspiration for right living. The American home must become again a center of learning how to live, as well as a center of living.

"Modern society is geared to a fast tempo; there are great demands on the parents to provide the material necessities for their children. Too often, the primary need for sympathetic and spiritual guidance is neglected and the child is deprived of the very element which is most essential to stabilize him emotionally and to aid him in his growth toward maturity. As a result of this thoughtless neglect, society suffers.

"What is needed is to restore the home to its proper place where the lessons of the Golden Rule are translated into daily living, where the members of the family counsel and aid each other, and where each has a share in the responsibilities of home life.

"What is needed is a return to the home where parents are companions of their children as well as the providers of the necessities of life, where parents share their leisure time with their children, and where children are taught the spiritual and civic responsibilities of manhood and womanhood. A child above all else needs the firm moral backing of a conscientious mother and father and the love, understanding, and security that a good Christian home affords.

"What is needed above all is to practice the living faith of our fathers in our daily lives and a dedication to making the Kingdom of God a reality on 'earth as it is in Heaven.'

"The neglect in the training of so many of our nation's youth, their lack of spiritual nourishment, their ignorance of the great truths of the Bible, and the tragic void of God and prayer in their lives weaken our homes and our nation's welfare."

Good Morals At Home

THE LORD EXPECTS his people to be pure in heart. That expectation includes every phase of our lives, our business and professional activities, our recreation and our most intimate relationships in the home.

No unclean thing can enter the kingdom of heaven, the Lord has said, and purity certainly must be considered a part of divinity.

The Lord taught us to love Him "with all thy mind" as well as with heart and might.

But can we love Him with all our mind unless our mind is pure?

And can we have a pure mind if we allow the evils of the world to remain in our thoughts, so that we dwell upon them?

Purity of thought is basic to purity of action. The thought gives birth to the act.

The relationship between husband and wife must always be one of purity. Commanded as we are to "multiply and replenish the earth," we are expected by the Lord to participate with Him righteously in one of the great creative acts by which He perpetuates life on earth.

The leaders of the Church have always taught that wives and mothers are the daughters of God, and should be so treated. They should not be subjected to perversion in any form.

Fathers and husbands are holders of the Holy Priesthood, and should carry with them a constant spirit of righteousness and purity, so that in their most intimate lives there will be no lust, no filth, and no imposition of uncleanness upon their wives.

Marriage is no license for uncleanness. There is no more justification for perversion after marriage than before marriage.

If we are to become "perfect as our Father in heaven is perfect," most assuredly we must build purity into our hearts and minds. As bearers of the vessels of the Lord, we must be clean.

President McKay at one time said:

"Man is endowed with appetites and passions for the preservation of his life and the perpetuation of his kind.

"These, when held under proper subjection, contribute to his happiness and comfort, but when used for mere gratification, lead to misery and moral degradation."

Again he said in referring to the divine quality of love:

"God has instituted marriage and the family as the proper condition of expressing in our lives this divine virtue. But sometimes men and women with low ideals and weakened wills permit their passions, like unbridled steeds, to dash aside judgment and self-restraint and to cause them to commit sin that may sear their conscience and leave in their hearts an everlasting regret.

"In this day when modesty is thrust into the background, and chastity is considered an outmoded virtue, I appeal to you to keep your souls unmarred and unsullied from this sin, the consequence of which will smite and haunt you intimately until your conscience is seared and your character sordid.

"Remember, too, the significance of the Savior's words saying that if any shall commit adultery even in his or her heart, he shall not have the Spirit but shall deny the faith, and shall fear.

"Resist evil and the tempter will flee from you.

"If you keep your character above reproach, no matter what others may think, or what charges they may make, you can hold your head erect, keep your heart light, and face the world undauntedly because you, yourself, and your God know that you have kept your soul untarnished."

And then President McKay adds:

"If marriage and home building be based upon physical attraction alone, love will sooner or later become famished and home life will be a heavy, disheartening existence."

Womanhood is divine. For any man to disgrace that womanhood is to debase himself. And for any husband to debase his wife is a beastly act in which there is anything but manhood.

Termites In The Home

As ONE OF our greatest advocates of good home life, President David O. McKay has said:

"If, upon examination, one finds that termites are undermining the foundations of his house, he should lose no time in having experts make a thorough examination and exterminate the destructive insects. He should have the weakened materials removed and the foundations strengthened, and if necessary rebuilt.

"But more important than the building of the house is the rebuilding and purifying of our homes. . . .

"There are destructive termites in homes as well as houses. Some of these are backbiting, evil speaking, faultfinding on the part of either parents or children.

"Slander is poison to the soul. Slanderers are like flies that pass over a man's good parts to light only on his sores.

"In the ideal home there is no slanderous gossip about school teachers, about public officials or Church leaders.

"I am more grateful now as the years have come and gone, to my father who said: 'No faultfinding about your teacher or anybody else.'

"Quarreling and profanity also are evils that lower the standards of the ideal home. I cannot imagine a father or mother profaning in the presence of children or ever letting profane words pass their lips.

"Another deterrent to happiness in the home is the refusal to bear the full responsibility of motherhood and fatherhood. Members of the Church who are healthy and normal should not be guilty of restricting the number of children in the home, especially when such action is prompted by a desire for a good time or for personal gain or to keep up with the neighbors, or by a false impression that one or two children in a family can be better educated. These are excuses which members of the Church should not harbor, for they are unjustified.

"The question of size of families, I know, brings up many problems — the question of woman's career, the false cry of quality not quantity, which one writer rightly says should read 'extinction not preservation,' or the matter-of-fact question of daily living and getting on in the world.

"With the high ideal of marriage as revealed to the Prophet Joseph Smith, members of the Church should have but one goal, and that is to keep in mind the fact that marriage, the foundation of society, is ordained of God, for the building of permanent homes in which children may be properly reared and taught the principles of the Gospel.

"All members of the Church should set their homes in order so that they may enjoy the true happiness of harmonious family life."

At another time, President McKay said:

"The low view of marriage that is gaining momentum throughout the world threatens civilization itself, and is contrary to the mind and will of God.

"To all really true men and women, children are their most precious possessions, and man's most important obligation and duty is the making of a home and the proper rearing of children.

"Marriage is a divine ordinance. It should not be entered into lightly nor terminated at pleasure.

"A clean body and uncontaminated blood are pre-requisites to an ideal marriage. The domestic relations precede and in our present existence are worth more than all other social ties.

"They give the first throb to the heart and unseal the deep foundations of its love. Its responsibilities, joys, sorrows, smiles, tears, hopes and solicitudes form the chief interests of human life."

Often President McKay has discussed the basic necessity of integrity.

"There is nothing in life so admirable as true manhood. There is nothing so sacred as true womanhood," he has said.

These foundations of a good home should never be eroded away. Like termites in a house, careless habits can soon weaken both manhood and womanhood, and when these are gone the meaning and purpose of home life are gone also.

And what is it that preserves manhood and womanhood and keeps the home intact?

It is the source of all strength of character — allegiance to God and his teachings.

If we live the Gospel of Jesus Christ in the home we preserve every quality of soul which holds marriages intact and builds these characteristics into the souls of the children.

The Gospel alone can provide the building stones of which a great home may be erected.

The Home Is First

MOST THOUGHTFUL PEOPLE were shocked at a recent police report on the relationship of the home to juvenile crime.

For years it has been supposed that teenage delinquency was mostly a result of broken homes. It seemed true for a long time, but it is not always the case.

The survey made by police officers revealed the astonishing fact that most juvenile crime reported in that study came from homes that were not broken. Furthermore they were listed as religious homes, and homes in which the mother did not go out to work.

This shattered many previous concepts about young people.

As reported in this newspaper: "The average first offense delinquent comes from a home with both parents, attends church, and has a non-working mother."

Sixty per cent of all delinquents included in this study came from so-called united homes, while only 28 per cent had divorced parents, and a mere six per cent had widowed mothers.

Of those studied as first offenders, 55 per cent were rated as being "active" in religion. Only one per cent reported having no religious affiliation.

What is the lesson for Church workers in this study?

Obviously it is that although young people may live in "religious" homes, they are not necessarily converted to their religion, and there is insufficient parental control over children to develop the kind of character traits which would persuade them to avoid crime.

Combined with parental neglect, even in "good" homes, there is of course the influence of crime on television, in movies, in magazines and newspapers, and a permissiveness both in school and at home which destroys proper restraints.

The false philosophy so widespread these days that it is wrong to correct or punish a child must likewise carry its share of the blame for criminality. Solomon is right, "Spare the rod and spoil the child."

The home life of each family deserves sincere study. Parents should ask themselves what they fail to do in properly rearing their children. They should keep in mind always the classic statement of President McKay: "No other success can compensate for failure in the home."

A great many parents are too busy for the good of their children. Some are too busy in Church work, some in business, some in social life. The fact is that many parents are taken out of the home so much that their children do not receive the attention and guidance they deserve.

Another study recently asked 100,000 children what they want most from their parents. As reported by Walt M. Lochman of Radio Station KMBZ in Kansas City, they listed the following do's and don'ts for parents:

1. Treat all of your children with equal affection.
2. Keep close to them.
3. Make their friends welcome in your home.
4. Don't quarrel in front of your children.
5. Be thoughtful of each other.
6. Never lie to the children.
7. Always answer their questions.

8. Don't punish them in the presence of other people.

9. Be constant in your affection and your moods.

10. Concentrate on good points, not so much on failings.

The Church is placing tremendous emphasis on the home at the present time, encouraging all members to develop better family life. It is most timely.

With the inroads of evil among all peoples, mothers and fathers must learn that the home is our greatest defense against crime and delinquency. But good homes mean more than an adequate income and comfortable surroundings, plenty to eat and a car to ride in.

Good homes must rate high in companionship between children and parents, in having a well-ordered household, with love between parents and between children and parents. They must build righteous loyalties, good character, a willingness to work, a spirit of humility and an absence of unjust pride, and they must teach a deep and abiding faith in God.

But like everything worthwhile, they require constant labor. Neither good homes nor strong families are achieved by wishful thinking or by remote control.

Tendency Towards Extremes

WHEN THE LORD taught that we should be temperate in all things, He gave us invaluable words of wisdom. There is a tendency on the part of nearly everyone to go to extremes in one way or another, so that often we lose the true perspective of life.

Extremes appear in almost every phase of our daily affairs. Some of us are extremists in health, others in religion; some take their occupations to the point where they shut out the rest of the world as they devote themselves almost exclusively to making money.

Some are extremists in child care, others in neglect of children; some carry what they call patriotism to unwise ends, while others defy genuine patriotism and undermine the body politic.

And so it goes. If only we could control ourselves that we might be "temperate in all things," we would live happier lives and give far more enjoyment to our associates.

Extremism is a costly thing. Take the mother for example who over-indulges her child. If the youngster is a daughter, the poor girl may never be allowed to live her own life. She may be "mothered" far beyond anything that is good for her, so that she never learns self-reliance and never makes a decision of her own.

If he is a son, the mother may so indulge him that he turns against parenthood in general, and women in particular. In one instance this sort of rebellion drove a son into a homosexual life in sheer defiance of all he had learned as he grew up.

And then there are fathers who drive their sons into delinquency and violence by constant nagging. A youngster may be left in a state of bewilderment because everything he does is called wrong and therefore he never learns what is right.

Well-meaning parents can make nervous wrecks of their own children by failing to control their tempers. They never find the important balance which only is obtained through "being temperate in all things."

Religious extremists at times drive their children into apostasy as youngsters are literally surfeited with a spiritual diet which, although tolerated at first, becomes repugnant with "over-doses" from unwise parents.

Political extremists sow seeds of hate and discord. Extremism among them can hardly be less dangerous on one hand than on the other. Both can lead to dictatorships.

Health faddists generally make themselves and other people uncomfortable. Instead of becoming the examples of good living they suppose themselves to be, at times they create quite the opposite effect.

Word of Wisdom extremists are much the same, never learning that there are other principles in the Gospel besides the fact that wheat is the staff of life. Do they never remember that what comes out of the mouth is far more important than what goes into it?

Style is another place where extremism occurs very frequently, often reaching the ridiculous.

Surely there must be a place for both modesty and good taste in manners and appearance.

It has been said that nothing is as uncommon as common sense. This certainly applies to the matter of extremism.

The Lord gave us good minds, and expects us to use them. He tells us that the glory of God is intelligence. He asks us to serve Him with all our minds.

One would suppose from this that He expects us to use our mentality to preserve a good balance of thought and action, and avoid the extremes which never fail to develop unhappiness and misery.

"Being temperate in all things" is good advice from Him who is most intelligent of all, and who has always placed justice and kindness, meekness and patience among the highest virtues.

See No Evil -- Think No Evil

IN THE UNITED States we have come to the point where seductive pictures, movies, books, magazines and all other pornographic items are in increasing demand.

In the name of freedom we have protected pornography in some of the courts, and have reached a point where honest citizens almost fear to expose crime because at times even our officials appear to protect it.

Pornography has reached Japan also. And as is true in America, immodest styles have made their impact upon Japanese morals.

This has been dramatically demonstrated in the recent moves in Japan to ape American and European styles in women's dress.

The *New York Times* recently reported that as hemlines have gone up in Japan, so has the ratio of sex crimes.

Only a small percentage of the women in Japan have come to wear hemlines above the knee, but even so sex crimes have doubled since the new styles came into vogue, according to reports of the Tokyo Metropolitan Police.

The police issued a report entitled "Miniskirts and Sex Crimes" which indicated that Tokyo's 2,627 sex crimes during the first nine months of 1967 doubled the number of similar offenses in the same period in 1966.

The police blamed the miniskirts.

The impact of pornographic styles, literature and films in America must be counted in similar terms. When has there been such a jump in sex crime as we now have in America? When has there been such delinquency on the part of both juveniles and their parents?

From as nearby as Boise, Idaho, we received a United Press report quoting the Ada County sheriff as saying, "Never before has there been such a breakdown in morals." He is asking for more money to run his office.

One of the most distressing reports on the breakdown of morals in America came in an Associated Press dispatch from New York reporting the attitude of 90 Episcopal priests, who held a day-long symposium, reaching the conclusion that homosexual activities are not immoral, and should not be condemned as such.

Thinking people are fast coming to the conclusion that there definitely is a world movement centered on wiping out morals.

When public officials seem to condone immorality, when courts refuse to handle obvious cases of guilt, when clergymen advocate a "new morality" which in truth is free love, and when styles go steadily deeper into the mire of exhibitionism, it should shock us into realizing that decent people must take steps to halt this malignant development.

There is an old advertising maxim which says: "Out of sight, out of mind." The reverse is also true. When we constantly portray the indecent and the unclean, we must expect a harvest in kind.

As hate begets hate and love begets love, so filth begets filth.

With all our present emphasis upon sex, now come the schools to add to the problem by introducing sex education in their classes.

It is true that many educators say that such instruction will reduce sex sin, but that is a fallacy. The sin nevertheless is on the increase, and frightfully so.

Parents must take a strong position to protect the morals of their children, but they must begin with themselves.

If all adults stayed away from "adults only" movies, there would be no such films to tempt children.

If all adults would voice their disgust with miniskirts which make exhibitionists out of so many of our girls and women, they could change this fashion.

If all adults would stop smoking and drinking, we would soon have a new generation which would not indulge in either vice.

If parents would but establish the kind of homes which nurture good character and cleanliness, most of our public problems would disappear.

How Late Is Too Late?

WHAT TIME IS a good time to get home from a date?

Who should decide?

What is a reasonable rule?

Many an unpleasant hour has been experienced in many a home because of a lack of understanding on these points.

Where is the path of wisdom in this matter, both from the standpoint of the youth and of patient parents who usually remain awake until everyone is in?

There is always a reasonable middle ground in these matters, and every Latter-day Saint, whether parent or youth, should earnestly strive to reach it for the best good of all.

Probably we should note in the first place that the hour of coming home should be and must be considered as a part of our over-all moral standard.

No one will question that our reputation, our character, our good name, and our standing before God are all related to it.

Too late can be tragic. Too early can cause hard feelings. How may we reach the happy middle ground?

Since parents and children are both concerned, both should have a voice in reaching the decision. The Church has always advised family council meetings as well as home evenings, when family matters may be discussed plainly and frankly, but in a spirit of love and cooperation.

There is no place for dictatorship in these family council meetings, any more than there is room for rebellion. But the final decision must rest with the parents.

One of the important things to be discussed is the age at which young people should begin to date.

For years the Church has advised against twosome dating at less than 16 years of age. Rather it has been urged that younger people go in groups, with proper chaperonage.

It is true that the "ways of the world" are at variance with that concept, but that does not make it wrong. The world has its standards, the Church sets up its own.

The world does not concern itself with morals in the same way in which the Church does, and is now accepting far lower standards than the Lord has ever been willing for His people to have. So we cannot follow the dictates of the world.

Then in our family council meeting, we should seek for the advice of the Lord and His Church. Since Latter-day Saints are believers and therefore obedient, we should do that which the Lord suggests.

He says: "Be ye temperate in all things." That means no extremes, either in demanding that we come in too early or that we remain out too late. He also said: "Retire to thy bed early," as will be remembered.

Too late or too early depends of course upon the age of the youngsters concerned. Certainly the early teenagers should be willing to recognize the curfew set up by law, which is 10 p.m. Since it is the law, let us observe it.

For older teenagers, what is reasonable?

The Church has set a good example to its members by closing its social activities by midnight, with the one exception of New Year's Eve, when special arrangements are made.

It is well known that many youngsters stay out past midnight, but is it a good idea? Is it even a good idea for older people?

Considering the next day's demands of both school and employment, is midnight too early? And then there is Saturday. This is the big night out for most wordly people. What about the Saints?

Sabbath Day observance is involved here. The Sabbath is still the Sabbath, even in the wee hours of the early morning. Should we not observe it? And is partying the thing to do on the Sabbath? Again midnight seems to be a good time to go home.

Critics call us prudish when we keep sensible hours; but they likewise use that epithet for those who won't smoke or drink, or neck or pet. Should their disparaging remarks be either persuasive or controlling?

The fact is that late hours are often directly related to moral problems of a serious nature.

Since Latter-day Saints are expected to protect their virtue, they should be willing to adopt habits which will assist them in doing so. Late hours can and often do break down moral restraints, which is always tragic.

If both parents and children will remember their Church standards, and if they will be reasonable with each other, they can easily reach an understandng on late hours which will meet the needs of all concerned.

Youngsters Ask Adult Aid

RHODE ISLAND STATE College was recently host to student delegates from 47 schools in that state at a "stop smoking" conference.

The young people held seminar classes with medical men, political leaders and newspaper and radio personalities in which they studied the results of smoking tobacco.

They made their own deductions too, the chief of which was:

"IF TEENAGERS ARE GOING TO STOP SMOKING, ADULTS MUST STOP TOO. IF SMOKING IS TO BE BANNED FOR STUDENTS IN SCHOOL, IT MUST BE BANNED FOR TEACHERS."

They admitted they are influenced by parents and other adults. They showed concern for the health of their parents. They said that no smoking education program for them will be effective until parents are reeducated too.

The students heard Dr. Ronald G. Vincent of the Roswell Park Memorial Institute in Buffalo, N.Y., talk of the facts that indicate cigarette smoking has accounted for epidemics of lung cancer, emphysema and heart ailments. They heard Representative John A. Fogarty outline the public health services' concern and plans for anti-smoking promotion.

The students discussed the facts with local doctors in small groups. The theme of the conference was "Too Tough to Care." Its aim was to give delegates facts and let them exchange ideas which they might use in their schools for programs that would lead to reduced smoking among youths.

The delegates made some suggestions but they also indicated some feeling of hopelessness. Most were not smokers.

More than one said, "How can we know what it will take to convince young people to stop smoking? What we have seen and heard today is frightening, but we were convinced before we came that smoking is bad."

The Providence (R.I.) *Evening Bulletin* devoted a full page to the convention.

In addition to pictures and news stories it reproduced a number of headlines carried previously in the same paper on news articles pertaining to smoking. Among these headlines were:

"Gov't. Warns Again of Smoking Dangers"

"Smoking Seen Cause of Fatal Fire"

"Epidemic Blamed on Cigarettes"

"R. I. Study Says Smoking Linked to Emphysema"

"One Type of Lung Cancer Linked Only to Cigarettes"

"Studies Say Smoking Rate Drops With Age"

"Doctor Finds Some Filters Don't Work"

"Analysis of Deaths Again Puts Finger on Cigarettes"

The appeal of the youngsters is a potent one. Parents must lead the way.

Adults set the pattern in the home.

Adults shape the thinking and the habits of their children.

Adults determine the social standards.

And adults write the laws.

If parents are determined to disregard the warnings, what chance do the children have?

The irresponsibility of smoking and drinking parents who give encouragement to their children to indulge in these habits is beyond understanding.

It is well recognized that most drinking teenagers admit that they had their first drink in their own homes.

Quoted in *Listen* magazine Dr. George Maddox, professor of medical sociology at Duke University, says that most drinking teenagers have their first drinks when between 12 and 14 years of age, and almost invariably in the home as their parents drink.

He said further that in a society where so many adults drink, the youngsters grow up thinking that the use of alcohol is a process of growing up. The same may be said about tobacco.

He added: "About one in four may become somewhat gay during a given month, and one in ten gets drunk. Most have confirmed their drinking patterns by the time they are 18 years of age."

The Greatest Force

"WHEN GOD WANTS a great work done in the world, or a great wrong righted, he goes about it in a very unusual way," wrote E. T. Sullivan.

"He doesn't stir up his earthquakes or send forth his thunderbolts.

"Instead he has a helpless baby born, perhaps in a simple home and of some obscure mother.

"And then God puts the idea into the mother's heart and she puts it into the baby's mind. And then God waits.

"The greatest forces in the world are not the earthquakes and the thunderbolts. The greatest forces in the world are babies."

And greater than the babies are the mothers who give them life and mold their thoughts and set their highest ideals. The hand that rocks the cradle is truly the hand that rules the world.

"Motherhood is the greatest potential influence either for good or ill in human life," said President David O. McKay.

"The mother's image is the first that stamps itself on the unwritten page of the young child's mind. It is her caress that first wakens a sense of security; her kiss, the first realization of affection; her sympathy and tenderness, the first assurance that there is love in the world."

President McKay also said: "The sweetness as well as the greatness of motherhood lies in the overcoming of self-love by Mother for her children. By nature the true mother is self-sacrificing. She is ever giving something of her life to make another either happier or better. Dying and giving — giving and dying — the two great elements that make the truly heroic — these are the Christlike virtues that make motherhood sublime.

"The beginning of motherhood is but the entrance into the valley of the shadow in order to bring life to another. Herein is manifest love supreme; for 'Greater love hath no man than this, that a man lay down his life for his friends.' (John 15:13.) That some women enter into this realm impelled by less lofty motives or uninspired by any self-sacrificing thought, there can be no doubt; but this fact cannot rob the truly heroic soul of the honor due her any more than the recreant soldier forced to the conflict can deprive of undying fame the hero who gloriously offers his life for his country.

"Motherhood is the one thing in all the world which most truly exemplifies the God-given virtues of creating and sacrificing. Though it carries the woman close to the brink of death, motherhood also leads her into the very realm of life and makes her co-partner with the Creator in bestowing upon eternal spirits, mortal life. Artists may make new visions real; poets express thoughts never known before or dress old ones in a more becoming garb; engineers may transform deserts into bounteous fields and fill them with prosperous towns and thriving villages; scientists may discover new elements and by various combinations thereof create means contributive either to progress or destruction — all these are in a measure revealers of unknown things; but the mother who, in compliance with eternal law, brings into the world an immortal spirit occupies first rank in the realm of creation.

"Motherhood is just another name for sacrifice. From the moment the wee, helpless babe is laid on the pillow beside her, Mother daily, hourly, gives of her life to her loved one. It has been aptly said that babes draw strength at first from her bosom but always from her heart. All through the years of babyhood, childhood, and youth, aye, even after her girls themselves become mothers and her sons, fathers, she tenderly, lovingly sacrifices for them her time, her comfort, her pleasures, her needed rest and recreation, and, if necessary, health and life itself! No language can express the power and beauty and heroism of a mother's love.

"For all this consecrated devotion, she asks nothing in return. If her love is reciprocated, she is content; but if not, and her wayward child with poisoned feelings turns heedlessly from her, she still loves on, giving in yearning and solicitude far more than the recreant deserves. No, she asks nothing in return; nothing for the roses she has transplanted from her own cheeks to those of her darling; nothing for the hours of vigilance during days and nights of sickness; nothing for the thousand self-denials and sacrifices that had to be made that the children in their 'teens' might receive proper schooling and 'appear well' with their comrades; nothing for the heartaches caused by thoughtless word or act of wayward youth.

"No, for all this and a thousand other things incident to motherhood, Mother asks nothing; but she deserves much. For kindness she deserves kindness; for tenderness, she should be given tenderness; for self-sacrifice, a little self-denial on the part of the children; for love, she should in return have love.

"In the most agonizing moment of His life, Christ thought of His mother. In this as in all other things, the Savior of men has given us an example. As Mother gave us our life 'at the peril of her own,' so we should be pleased, no matter what our desires, our condition, or our pains, to give such of our time, our thought, our words, our means, as may be necessary to Mother's contentment and peace.

"To each Mother's son or daughter, we would say: You need no suggestions on how to make your mother happy on Mother's Day as on every day of the year. If you order a white carnation to be given her, she will be pleased; if you tell her in a letter of your appreciation and love, she will shed tears of happiness; but if you keep the spotless character and purity of soul she has given you, she will rejoice as the most blessed of mothers."

Temple Marriage
For Salvation

WHEN THE GOSPEL was restored, it was brought back to earth in its fulness. It provided the saving ordinances as well as divine principles of salvation.

In restoring the Gospel, the Lord set up a Church which was new to the modern world. It borrowed nothing from any other church, but was distinctly different in that in its entirety it was literally brought back from heaven.

It provided the way of life, and those who accepted it were expected to live according to its program.

The Lord introduced His own saving ordinances and restored divine authority to perform them, thus making them valid.

For example, He provided that baptism could be performed in only one way. It had to be by immersion as a symbol of the death and resurrection of the Savior. But even immersion alone was not enough. It was meaningless without the divine authority to make it acceptable to heaven.

As the Lord established His own mode of baptism, so He introduced His own mode of marriage. It is generally spoken of as temple marriage.

Temple marriage is an ordinance of the Gospel, a saving ordinance without which we cannot obtain exaltation in the kingdom of God.

It is as much a saving ordinance as baptism or the laying on of hands. We can no more set it aside than we can turn away from baptism or the Sabbath.

It is a law of God which all hoping to receive His highest blessings must obey.

Latter-day Saints of course recognize civil marriage, for no marriage is a marriage unless it complies with the laws of the land.

Temple marriage is "civil" too in the sense that it is legal and fully recognized by the law of the land.

But it is far more than a civil marriage. It is a marriage for eternity as well, allowing a man and wife and children to perpetuate their family living into the eternities.

But it is even more than that. It is the means of obtaining still further blessings and endowments without which we cannot be exalted.

Some who postpone temple sealings until they learn whether their civil marriage is to be successful, forget that the temple marriage includes more than the marriage itself and that they forfeit these additional blessings so essential to exaltation if they marry out of the temple.

A Justice of the Peace cannot provide God's mode of marriage because his authority is limited to the law of the land.

Bishops and stake presidents cannot provide it either, for their marriages also are limited to the law of the land. Their marriages, of course, are under the influence and atmosphere of the Church, which is always desirable, but not even these Church officers can perform a temple marriage. They do not have that authority.

Only a certain few men on earth are given the sealing power to bind on earth and in heaven, and they alone can perform temple marriages.

It was so in the early Christian Church. It is the same today.

Temple marriage is related to a fulness of the Priesthood of which President Joseph Fielding Smith once said: "There is no exaltation in the Kingdom of God without a fulness of the Priesthood. The Prophet Joseph Smith has said: 'If a man get a fulness of the Priesthood of God he has to get it by keeping all the commandments of God and obeying all the ordinances of the House of the Lord.'

"Every man who is faithful and will receive these ordinances and blessings obtains a fulness of the Priesthood. The Lord has made it possible for every man in this Church through his obedience to receive the fulness of the Priesthood through the ordinances of the Temple of the Lord. They cannot be obtained anywhere else."

Women cannot receive their higher blessings anywhere else either, for those blessings are conferred upon men and women jointly as they kneel at the marriage altar. All of course is conditioned upon faithfulness.

We read in Section 131 of the Doctrine and Covenants: "In the celestial glory there are three heavens or degrees; and in order to obtain the highest, a man must enter into this order of the priesthood [meaning the new and everlasting covenant of marriage]; and if he does not, he cannot obtain it."

It is the same for women as for men. The man is not without the woman, neither is the woman without the man in the Lord.

God's Wisdom--And Man's

THE LORD HAS taught that His ways are not man's ways. This has been proven repeatedly, but man still ignores it.

The world will soon discover this to be true also in the present movement to control births.

The United States is taking a leading role in the development and dissemination of birth control information and devices, not only here at home, but worldwide.

Only a few weeks ago through the Agency for International Development, our country provided a half million dollars' worth of oral contraceptives to India, enough to supply 100,000 women with pills for 18 months.

Major birth control programs are now under way in scores of countries, largely fostered by American interests.

In India 5 per cent of the women are now taking "the pill," as do 6 per cent of the women in Pakistan, 20 per cent in Korea, 13 per cent in Taiwan, and 11 per cent in Hong Kong and Singapore. Throughout Central and South America there are similar extensive private and governmental programs.

It is estimated that 14 million women in the world now take "the pill," half of them being Americans. The effect as yet has not appeared to any extent in the vital statistics. There are still 14 million babies born each year in India.

Generally the reason given for this widespread adoption of birth control is the shortage of food. More recently some have attempted to justify it by saying that although the pill is fatal to some women, these deaths are not as numerous as those from forced abortions; therefore by birth control more lives are saved.

Nations now, however, are beginning to liberalize abortion laws, apparently in the hope of reducing the birth rate in two ways — using more pills and inducing more abortions.

In this birth control effort man places himself in direct opposition to the plan and laws of God.

The Almighty made this world, and He made us. All human beings are His children, His spirit offspring, and it is His intention to provide each one of us with a body of flesh and bones. This body is essential to eternal progress.

With this in mind He gives us the powers of procreation and permits us to join with Him in a divinely sponsored act.

But by preventing or aborting legitimate births, we oppose this plan.

His spirit children are born into bodies of flesh and bones by His own design.

Then who are we to prevent it?

Are we so naive as to believe that God would fail to provide for His own offspring as they come into the world? That would be to regard the Infinite as being less considerate than finite mortals.

Many people point to the starving millions of India and China. But why are they starving? Is it because the earth cannot produce sufficient food for all its inhabitants? Or is poor management by imperfect man to blame?

It seems appropriate for us to begin to revise upward our conception of the wisdom and power of the Infinite.

In speaking of the fulness of the earth, the Almighty told the Prophet Joseph Smith that there is "enough and to spare."

Agriculturalists frequently remind us that if proper farming methods were used, the earth could and would produce "enough and to spare" for all mankind.

Governments and private groups would do well to study the word of God, understand His plan for His children, and reconstruct their faith in Him.

He will provide, if we but obey Him. He who has made the deserts to blossom as the rose, and who has promised that abundant waters will spring forth in the "thirsty place" and that He will care for His faithful children, can give to the earth the abundance of its paradisiacal verdure.

And consider those of us who live in America — where is the justification for widespread birth control here? Is this country in danger of starvation? Are we over-populated? Or do we have a more selfish reason for using half the world's contraceptives?

God says: "Multiply and replenish the earth."

He has not revoked that commandment, but He has promised us "enough and to spare" if we follow His teachings.

Why not begin to believe Him?

"Gun Shy" About Movies

A MOTION PICTURE editor recently carried a startling story saying that a certain very filthy film drew five times the patronage of a so-called "family picture," and then added: "Are wholesome films wanted?"

He said: "If 'Young Americans' were a poorly produced film, there would be a reason for its failure at the box office. But it is well made from every angle. It tells, in a fascinating way, how the first Young Americans singing group was organized, and then follows them on a fun-filled tour of the U.S."

After further lamenting the poor patronage for this film, and explaining that it ran in a local theater only for one week, he asked: "Where are the movie-goers who say they want wholesome pictures?"

This editor's report should be regarded as a warning to movie producers, rather than as a commentary on the public taste.

It is admittedly regrettable that large numbers of people are so depraved in their tastes that they patronize filth wherever it is found. But it is quite as sad that producers of smut are willing to make their living out of corrupting public morals.

The movie makers completely "miss the boat" when they suppose that the public does not like clean, family-type films. Are their memories so short that already they have forgotten what "Sound of Music" did for them? It packed the theaters in record runs, and made millions for the producers. And likewise "To Sir, With Love," one of the best pictures in years.

The problem is not that the public does not want good films. The real difficulty is that the decent segment of society (and thank heaven they are still in the majority) no longer trusts either the movie makers or their advertising, and are afraid to expose their children to the filth so often and so unexpectedly placed before their eyes under the guise of innocence.

It may seem strange for a newspaper writer to say that certain kinds of advertising cannot be trusted, but a great many people are now beginning to feel that way.

Read any movie ad, and try to tell what the picture is like!

When people do not come to their theaters, the movie industry itself is to blame, as are also the advertising men.

Advertising writers seem to have the idea that they must put sex into every ad they write. This goes not only for movies, but for almost everything else from automobile tires to kitchen stoves.

Clean people are sick and tired of it. Therefore they distrust these ads, and turn away from them.

When parents see a display of sex in a movie advertisement they immediately suppose that the picture is another portrayal of perversion, and refrain from taking their children to see it. This they do entirely as a means of self-protection, not that they wouldn't like to take their youngsters to a good movie. They are becoming scared of the movies!

Good pictures have been poorly billed in their advertising, and this will account largely for the failure of such films to receive public support.

But so many bad pictures have been given an innocent look, that parents have become very hesitant about taking their children to see any of them.

When movies like "Sound of Music" and "To Sir, With Love" make such good money, shouldn't the movie makers be willing to make even more money by producing more pictures of the same caliber? Wasn't that a lesson to them? What other picture has had the length of run enjoyed by "Sound"?

Can "Hell's Chosen Few," or "Sex and the Single Girl" or "Touched by Temptation" or "Have Figure, Will Travel" or "Planet of the Apes" or any others of their ilk even begin to compare with it?

Even "Gone With the Wind" had to be given a sex slant in the ads!

The public wants clean movies all right, but it is sated with misrepresentations of what is good and what is not.

If honest-to-goodness clean family pictures of a high quality were made and properly advertised they would enjoy good business.

But when filth is peddled as extensively as it now is, sensible parents just naturally become "gun-shy" of ALL films, and as a means of protecting their families from the corrupting influence found in so many theaters, they stay away in droves.

Let the movie industry "come clean" with the public and the public will respond. The psychology that to be popular, a thing must be filthy, is about as wrong as our guesses on how to fight the war in Vietnam.

The majority of our population is still clean, and they want to remain that way and rear their children in a wholesome atmosphere.

Joseph, The Seer Of God

IN A FEW days we will reach the anniversary of the birth of Joseph Smith, the seer of latter days.

In complete fulfillment of the prediction of Moroni to Joseph, the name of the latter-day prophet has indeed been heard for good or ill the world around.

But now there is greater honor ascribed to him than previously. With the growing strength of the Church and the increased understanding of the true mission of Joseph Smith, more and more people recognize him for what he truly was — a prophet of God.

Time has been on the side of the Prophet Joseph. As the years have gone by, and new knowledge has been made available through scholarly research, and as men have become sated with medieval views so unsuited to the age in which we now live, a new day has dawned for the world.

In a little more than a century, mankind has come to recognize a fact for which Joseph Smith was persecuted most. He said there has been a departure from original Christianity.

No one in possession of the facts any longer believes that the Gospel as given by the Savior when he was in mortality has existed in its purity down through the ages.

No well-informed person now thinks that the Church organization as established by the Savior in mortality has survived the centuries.

Everyone who knows the facts recognizes and acknowledges now that there has been a tremendous change in the views, doctrines and organization of Christian churches as the years have rolled on.

And they recognize the need of returning to Christ's basic doctrines!

Hence the ecumenical councils which have been held; hence the public statements of high church officials that religions long since considered infallible and unchangeable, now must be altered to more nearly resemble the teachings of the Bible.

It was most significant that one of the world's great religious leaders, associated with a church whose claims to infallibility have persisted over the centuries, now announces that his church must be brought back to Christ and the Bible.

Critics of Joseph Smith argued a hundred years ago that Mormonism could not be true because it refuted some of the basic tenets of Christian faith. Today these tenets are being revised to teach the very things which Joseph taught.

Ancient documents, such as the Dead Sea Scrolls and others recently found by archaeologists, are opening the Bible to a new understanding, compelling scholars within certain churches to insist on readjustments, since the old views are no longer tenable.

There is even talk in some churches about a restoration of true Gospel principles, and one large denomination is talking in terms of seeking new revelation, a thing for which Joseph was roundly condemned by persecutors who finally accomplished his death.

Joseph Smith taught true Christian doctrine on a comprehensive scale, touching many subjects, including principles of astronomy and other sciences, although he was neither an astronomer nor a scientist.

And yet much of the latest scientific research gives endorsement to what he taught a hundred years ago.

Who in Joseph's day knew about space? Joseph did, and his writings harmonize with scientific teachings of today.

Who knew about the evils of tobacco in Joseph's day? But science knows now.

Who even spoke of other worlds being inhabited? Joseph did in his day. Only now are some scientific men interested in this subject. Our Venus-probes and Mars-probes are but part of a program to find this truth. And flying saucers? Joseph didn't talk about them, but men do today — thinking that other planets are sending expeditions to study the earth. And how could they do this if other orbs were not inhabited?

Joseph said other worlds are inhabited, and by the children of God!

His doctrines of salvation, our relationship to God, the fact of a divine creation, our personal destinies, bring increasing comfort to all who know them.

With each passing year, the stature of Joseph Smith increases. The perspective of time places an ever more convincing stamp of divinity upon his work.

He was the Prophet of God.

Eccentric Or Right?

DURING ONE OF our wars we sang a popular song about an ineffective soldier who couldn't even march.

But there was a proud mother who saw only good in her son, and as the soldiers paraded by, she sang:

"And they're all out of step but Jim."

Sometimes this can be literally true. They can all "be out of step but Jim" in certain matters.

Recently an English newspaper, commenting upon a TV production telling of the "Mormon Invasion" of Great Britain, carried this comment among others:

"Eccentric they must certainly be accounted. They believe in the literal truth of the Old Testament."

It was a new way of putting it. Maybe believers in the Old Testament are eccentric in the eyes of those who relegate it to the realm of mythology.

And likewise those who believe in the New Testament, with the life and miracles of Christ including His death and resurrection, may also be classed as eccentrics by the same critics. And from their warped point of view, it probably is so.

Many today, particularly in Europe, seriously question the authenticity of the scriptures, not only of the Old Testament, which some regard as a fairy tale, but of the life and works of the Savior.

One of England's leading clerics, in an address before a group of divinity students at a British university, spoke of the miracles of Christ, and said: "They indeed were wonderful — if they ever happened."

With the clergy taking this attitude, and the populace willing to follow, it is no wonder that the Mormon elders are considered by some to be eccentric.

But are they?

It will be remembered that in Jesus' own day He was considered eccentric by the scribes and Pharisees, some of whom said He was a devil.

And John the Baptist was regarded as an eccentric. He ate locusts!

And Paul before Festus was told that much learning had made him mad. So he too was considered an eccentric.

George Washington was considered an eccentric by his loyalist enemies. Ben Franklin was thought by many to be eccentric. He played with a kite and a key and a flash of fire that came out of the sky!

And Alexander Bell. What a strange man, trying to make sound pass along a telephone wire! And Marconi? Only a fool could believe that sound could be transmitted by air, it was said.

When everyone thought the world was flat, how eccentric could a man be who taught that it was in reality round?

Eccentric?

Have those, who point the finger, ever thought that the "eccentric" might be right? Was Franklin wrong? Was Bell or Marconi? Was Paul mad? Was John the Baptist a misguided wayfarer, crying in the wilderness?

Jesus told the Prophet Joseph Smith not to join any of the churches, for they were all wrong. That put them all "out of step."

Joseph Smith was commissioned to organize the one and only true Church of Jesus Christ on earth in modern times. That made them all out of step but him!

The Mormon elders now teach in lands dominated by churches which existed in the day when Joseph went into the woods to pray. Their doctrines differ from the creeds of the existing churches. That makes the elders different, admittedly. Possibly that constitutes a definition of the eccentric.

But the elders have the truth. God spoke to Joseph Smith. The true Church is again upon the earth.

It had to be different from all other churches. It had to teach a doctrine which was strange in the midst of the popular man-made creeds of the world.

If this is being eccentric, then so be it.

And they are all "out of step but Jim."

Guided By Prophets

WHEN PEOPLE ASK how we differ from other Christians, they are given various reasons.

. But one stands out: We are guided by revelation through modern prophets.

Without modern revelation there would be no Mormonism. Without modern prophets we could hardly distinguish ourselves from other Christian groups.

This typical doctrine causes some criticism and at times ridicule on the part of those who no longer believe in current revelation since it has been lacking for so many centuries.

We are told that the heavens are sealed as brass over our heads and that there can be no more revelation.

This is indeed the line of demarkation. But it was mankind who sealed the heavens — not the Almighty. He is always ready to hear and bless His faithful people.

At no time has He sealed the heavens — but, rather, the iniquities of the people have done so. It was the case even in Isaiah's time, for he gave this explanation:

"Behold, the Lord's hand is not shortened, that it cannot save; neither his ear heavy that it cannot hear: But your iniquities have separated between you and your God, and your sins have hid his face from you." (Isaiah 59.)

When men supplanted revelation with their own wisdom, when they allowed wordly power to eliminate spiritual direction, of course God ceased speaking to them. Of course the heavens closed. But humans were the cause of it.

Has He not always promised to answer prayer? Has He not always spoken through prophets when the people listen? And has He not always said that He would do nothing "but he revealeth his secret unto his servants the prophets"?

If He will not act except through His prophets, then prophets become basic officers in His Church. And revelation likewise becomes equally necessary, for how can prophets act unless God reveals Himself to them?

It is this vital principle which was lost to the world over the centuries, resulting in the spiritual darkness which has continued until recent times.

Why should people revile against prophecy? It would be their salvation if they would accept it.

Why do they revile against the prophets? Why have they done so through past ages?

They reviled anciently because they resented having their works of darkness exposed. Some do the same today. But others reject modern prophecy simply because they do not know what it is, never having lived in the presence of a living oracle.

But now come new prophets in the earth. They are inspired men, some of whom have seen God and talked with Him; others who constantly receive the dictation of His Holy Spirit.

In the Restored Church, this principle of prophecy exists as the outstanding evidence of its divinity. And in this Church, together with prophecy, are the other spiritual gifts known for so long in ancient times, but for such a lengthy period lost from among us.

The Lord is kind, and one of the chief manifestations of His goodness is His communication with mankind, which always comes through His prophets.

What better could the Almighty do for us than to speak to us, give us guidance, light and intelligence? What more could He do than to pour out His spirit upon all flesh as Joel said, and provide an enlightened age such as we now have?

What more could He do than to provide for us the raw materials for a great civilization and brightness of mind to develop them?

What more could He do than to give direction through inspired prophets who teach us how to become like Him?

As general conferences come and go, we note an increased outpouring of His spirit, an ever-growing inspiration to guide us into ways of success, so that we may enjoy the abundant life.

The entire Church pauses at conference time to listen to the men whom God has placed at the head of His Church, and we invite all mankind everywhere to do likewise.

"Come, listen to a prophet's voice, and hear the word of God."

The Prophet And President

THROUGHOUT THE CHURCH there is a rapidly increasing tendency to speak of President David O. McKay as "the Prophet." And rightly so.

In each age when the Lord has had a people on earth, He has guided them by revelation. Always that revelation has come through a living prophet. While urging the people to "search the scriptures" and profit by the advice He had given anciently, the Lord nevertheless gave current direction for the present day.

This is one of the outstanding elements of the restoration of the Gospel. The principle of prophecy has been restored. But it was not given merely that future events might be foretold, for such is hardly the whole field of prophecy. Probably more important than giving predictions is providing the day-by-day divine guidance which we need.

Conditions vary from time to time, making continuous guidance necessary. It was never the intent of the Lord to leave His people groping in the dark, but to give them light and direction to help them live successfully, and this He has given through His anointed servants.

Anciently Amos said appropriately: "Surely the Lord God will do nothing, but he revealeth his secret unto his servants the prophets."

On the day the Church was organized, the Lord gave a revelation to the Prophet Joseph Smith reestablishing the official status of the Prophet for this day.

He decreed that the president of the Church should be His prophet, seer and revelator, as well as His inspired translator when such service was required.

The Lord at that time told the Church membership that if they would hearken to His prophet and follow his directions "as if from mine own mouth," they would be preserved and prospered in their lives.

President McKay is the Prophet for this day. He is the Lord's mouthpiece now. He gives us the divine guidance which the Lord has for us presently living.

With him are his counselors, also sustained as prophets, seers and revelators, and the Council of the Twelve. These men, in their apostolic callings, are entitled to the revelation of God for their respective assignments.

A visitor once asked what distinguished the Latter-day Saints from other Christians. The reply he received was: "Prophecy."

The stranger in our midst did not understand. Then it was explained to him that God in our day has restored all that was had anciently among the people.

Probably the outstanding characteristic of ancient Israel was that prophets ministered among them. This was true also of the early Christian Church. Christian prophets were placed in the Church by the Savior Himself even as prophets were given in Old Testament times.

When the visitor was told that "prophecy" was the mark of distinction, he was taught in effect that the Latter-day Saints are different because here and now they receive the guidance of the Almighty. To them the heavens are not sealed. Although they accept the Bible as the word of God, they don't believe it contains ALL of his revelations.

In modern times, people need heavenly guidance as much as did those who lived anciently. That guidance is not to come through those who "peep and mutter," nor by mysterious uncertain tactics traditionally handed down through the ages.

As Paul said, God does not work "in a corner." He is open and what He does is in harmony with scripture.

His way of communicating with His people was known to everyone anciently. All knew the prophet. Many consulted him, even on political matters. His word was accepted "as if from mine own mouth."

This gift He restored in modern times. The Church now is headed by prophets, with the President as the leader of them all. Today that man is President McKay.

He holds the powers which the angels bestowed upon the Prophet Joseph Smith. He has the same authority held by Peter, James and John; by John the Baptist, Moses, Elijah, Noah, and others who came as angels — even "divers other angels," as explained by Joseph Smith.

The presidents of the Church today are among the greatest of all the prophets. Who but they have held all the authorities and powers of all former times?

And at the head of this unique but vast organization is President McKay, our leader for today, our prophet, God's seer, our esteemed friend and co-laborer.

God strengthen him for his every duty!

"As If From Mine Own Mouth"

THE PRINCIPLE OF prophecy is vital to the religion of the Latter-day Saints. Without it they would have no religion.

The principle provides that at the head of the Church there shall be a prophet sustained by faithful people as the mouthpiece of God, and that in fact this prophet shall be a revealer of the divine will.

It is for him to point the way for the people of God. And it is for the people to follow him "in all patience and faith."

The scriptures from Genesis to Revelation bear this out. And they portray the results of obedience to or defiance of this principle.

Certainly "where there is no vision the people perish." But where there is vision — and wisdom to follow it — there is progress, peace and prosperity.

The people of Moses' day had both their prophet and their flesh-pots. It was easy for them to yearn for their former security and to rebel against their prophet when all did not go to please them.

But who had the greater vision, the vacillating people or the inspired prophet? Where was their true security, in their flesh-pots or in their divinely appointed leader?

In the days of King Ahab the people had their Jezebels and their state security. But they also had both Elijah and Elisha. In whom did they prosper?

Were the Corinthians better off following Paul or in going after the dissenters who splintered them into divisive groups?

Is it any different today?

Once again there are prophets on earth. Once again God has spoken, even as He did to Moses and Abraham. There are revelators on the earth again! Inspired direction by means of the visions of holy men is once again available to the people!

It started in our time with the Prophet Joseph Smith. On the day the Church was organized, the Lord revealed anew His ancient principle of directing His people by prophecy.

As He appointed Joseph Smith, He said: "Thou shalt be called a seer, a translator, a prophet, an apostle of Jesus Christ, an elder of the church through the will of God the Father, and the grace of your Lord Jesus Christ, being inspired of the Holy Ghost." (D&C 21.)

This is the calling of the President of the Church. Joseph was the first President of this restored Church, and the keys and powers of his appointment were transmitted to each of his successors. They too are and have been seers, prophets, apostles, revelators, men of vision and inspired foresight.

To make certain that the people would fully understand the position to which He appointed their President, the Lord said in further explanation: "Wherefore, meaning the church, thou shalt give heed unto all his words and commandments which he shall give unto you as he receiveth them, walking in all holiness before me.

"For his word ye shall receive AS IF FROM MINE OWN MOUTH, in all patience and faith."

Can there be any misunderstanding that language? Can the people fail to know from this the great obligation they have to follow the inspired word of their President?

But the commandment is not without promise, and the promise is vital to the welfare of all the people as well as to each individual:

"For by doing these things the gates of hell shall not prevail against you; yea, and the Lord God will disperse the powers of darkness from before you, and cause the heavens to shake for your good, and his name's glory."

The path of safety for the Saints always has been in following their President. We are divinely promised that the President will never lead the Church astray.

In this day of confusion, pressures, rebellion and sin, dare God's people ignore God's word?

Counting Our Many Blessings

LATTER-DAY SAINTS HAVE much to be thankful for this year.

The Church is growing more rapidly than ever before. Membership world-wide will soon reach the three million mark. During the past approximately 12 years the population of the Church has doubled. In the last half century it has multiplied five times. In the lifetime of President McKay it has multiplied twenty times!

The young people of the Church, contrary to the world-wide trend, for the most part are clean and virtuous, upholding the standards of the Church.

They do not riot, they do not resist their patriotic duties, and they do not resort to the "new morality" which now attracts the rest of the world. They regard virtue as more important than life.

Our young people love the Gospel. More of them now study it daily than ever before. Attendance at seminaries and institutes climbs spectacularly.

Student wards organized near many large universities are among the most active in the Church. Most of them average 75 per cent Sacrament meeting attendance. The great majority of the members of these wards are active. These young people, although they are earnestly engaged in their educational activities, nevertheless find time to serve the Lord.

Temple marriages are at a high point. Statistics on this subject are pleasing to bishops and stake presidents, for they show in no uncertain terms the faithfulness of the youth of Zion.

Auxiliaries are steadily improving their programs and increasing their effectiveness.

Sacrament meeting attendance world-wide is higher than ever before. Fast offerings reach a higher figure, and more people today are paying an honest tithing than ever before in the history of the Church.

The attitude of the world toward the Church is greatly improved, despite certain occasional outbreaks written by prejudiced or ill-informed individuals. The great publications of the nation continue to provide favorable publicity for the Church.

The Hill Cumorah pageant is now heralded as the greatest religious spectacle in America. It attracts audiences in excess of a hundred thousand every year, playing more nights and to more people than ever before.

General conference reaches all around the world. More radio stations and TV networks carry conference services than ever before, while short-wave carries the Gospel almost daily to remote parts of the earth.

The number of wards, stakes and missions continues to increase. People of high intellectual attainment are more and more being attracted to the Church, while the great middle class continues to provide the fibre which makes any organization great.

The programs of the Church reach into more areas of life than before. The Welfare Program is more extensive, more efficient each year.

The musical progress of the Church continues onward. The Tabernacle Choir sings before more groups in conventions and other important functions than ever, and the radio still carries it as one of the greatest continuing programs of all time.

Home life is being emphasized as never before. Home evenings become a part of the regular habits of the Saints. Home teaching brings more people into activity. Fellowship programs attract new converts and hold their interest.

The leadership of the Church, under the inspired direction of living prophets of God, point an unerring course to the future, where joy, happiness and security may be found by faithful Saints regardless of world conditions.

While the worldly doubt more and more, the faith of the Latter-day Saints increases. The testimony of Jesus is the most outstanding characteristic of the Church.

Latter-day Saints testify to all mankind that indeed God does live, for their prophets have seen Him; that Jesus is the Christ, and that He has inaugurated a modern ministry; that the Latter-day Saints are the servants of God, for He has given them His restored Gospel.

For all of God's choice blessings, the Latter-day Saints express their humble gratitude to a most gracious and kind Heavenly Father.

The Way To The Truth

Most people are good people. Most believe in God, and most have an earnest desire to serve Him.

Although the headlines tell of the wicked, who by their violence win the most publicity, the vast majority of people are good.

In their desire to serve God, often they frankly admit they do not know how to do so. They are confused by the many diversified opinions about religion. There are many denominations, all claiming to be right.

How can the honest observer know which Church is right, and which will provide for him the assurance of salvation if he obeys?

The scripture leaves many marks of identification by which the average person may know how to recognize the true Church.

One of the unexpected marks of identification is the name by which the members of the Church were known anciently. They were not at first called Christians, neither were they Protestants or Catholics. They were called Saints, as is shown in various parts of holy writ. This name was applied to the entire Church membership, not to the few.

The Church was marked by current revelation which came to holy prophets ministering among the people. Most agree that there were prophets in Old Testament times, but few think of them as being part of the organization of the Christian Church.

But as Paul explains in Ephesians, Christ gave both apostles and prophets to be ministers in the Christian Church, to remain in it until we reach perfection. Where are the prophets and apostles of modern Christendom?

And where is the current revelation?

This is especially important so far as the Christian clergy is concerned, as well as being vital to the welfare of the people. Ministers for Christ are to be called of God as was Aaron (Heb. 5:4) and Aaron was called by current revelation to a living mortal prophet. If that is the pattern, we see more than ever that prophets are necessary to receive the revealed word of God appointing men to the ministry. Only in this way can men be "called of God as was Aaron."

This is one of the most important of all signs of the true Church.

But what is another? It is closely related both to prophets and revelation. It is the production of new scripture as additions to already existing scripture. It was in this way we obtained the Bible. Prophets received revelations; they recorded them, and the records became scriptures.

In all ages God speaks through His prophets. "Surely the Lord God will do nothing, but he revealeth his secret unto his servants the prophets," said Amos, If prophets are to be in the Christian Church, and are to receive revelation, it is only to be expected that they would record those revelations, which then would become scripture. In this way new and additional scripture is provided for the people.

Where is the Christian Church which provides new scripture, through new revelation to modern prophets?

Many other signs of the true Church might be mentioned. But these are sufficient to call attention to some of the basic characteristics.

Our souls are most precious. Each of us should be vitally interested in his own salvation.

When the Lord was on earth He clearly taught (Matt. 15) that we cannot be saved by the precepts of man.

Only God's word will save. Uninspired creeds may be the work of sincere men, it is true, but when those men no longer believe in revelation from God, saying that the Bible contains it all, how can they expect to deliver God's will?

Salvation is so important to us that we must learn which is God's way and distinguish it from man's precepts, remembering that there is but one Lord, one faith (or religion) and one baptism.

The Lord organized only one Church. Paul taught that Christ is not divided. Denominationalism is division. The denominations of today run into the hundreds. Which one is right?

"Indifferentism"-- No. 1

As LONG AGO as the days of Peter and Paul, even back into Old Testament times, indifferent attitudes toward Gospel truths have been combated by advocates of revealed religion.

The "don't care" attitude which is so common today is nothing new. Neither is it confined to matters of religion. But always it is the enemy of him who possesses it. It spells retrogression and destruction.

Did any great man ever achieve preeminence by a "don't care" attitude? Did the "don't care" individual ever graduate from college with honors, or make the football team, or become President of the United States?

Those who care are those who achieve, and those who care obtain results.

Whereas the "don't care" attitude is fatal, spiritually speaking, for those who pay no heed to Gospel teachings, it is nearly as difficult for those within religious groups who don't care to which denomination they belong, or to which baptism they subscribe, or who say that it doesn't matter whether one belongs to any church at all, if he lives a moral and honest life.

One cannot be honest with himself by retaining these views.

With Christ, there is a stand to take, a line to follow, a dedication to accept.

It was He who taught that there is but one way, a single straight gate, one fold and one Shepherd. It was Paul who taught "one Lord, one faith, and one baptism," and who asked in all candor: "Is Christ divided?"

Comforting as it may seem to some to believe that any creed will do, it nevertheless is a false notion. It was not so with Christ.

The Savior made this plain as He spoke to the Pharisees of His day (Matt. 15) and clearly taught that uninspired precepts of men will not save, neither will old traditions nor long cherished dictums.

The new "Jerusalem Bible" translation makes this even more clear than does the King James version, and says:

"The worship they offer me is worthless; the doctrines they teach are only human regulations."

In the rendering given in Mark 7:6-9 this version says: "This people honors me only with lip service while their hearts are far from me. The worship they offer me is worthless; the doctrines they teach are only human regulations. You put aside the commandment of God to cling to human traditions. And He said to them — How ingeniously you get around the commandment of God in order to preserve your own tradition . . . You make God's word null and void for the sake of your tradition which you have handed down. And you do many other things like this."

The Authentic New Testament sustains the Jerusalem (Catholic) Bible. "It is useless for them to worship me while teaching as doctrine, injunctions of men."

The New English Bible says: "Their worship of me is in vain, for they teach as doctrines the commandments of men."

Every person has his free agency, and each one is entitled to worship in whatever way he chooses. But he must remember that some forms of worship, as indicated above by the Savior, cannot provide salvation.

Indifference to religion is deadly, both spiritually and morally, and largely has been responsible for the widespread immorality, crime and corruption which face us today.

But indifference to the kind of religion is equally misleading. If Christ is not divided, there can be no division over the necessity of baptism, for Christ commanded it. There can be no division as to the mode of baptism, because only immersion is a baptism. There can be no division as to authority, for only those called by current revelation through a living prophet are authorized servants of God. (Heb. 5:4.)

The world is endeavoring to heal the wounds of denominationalism through ecumenical movements. But only an acceptance of the principle of "one Lord, one faith (or religion) and one baptism" can bring it about.

And that Lord must be Jesus Christ. That faith must be His Gospel IN ITS PURITY, untrammeled by man-made innovations, and that baptism must be that with which the Savior himself set the example. There is only one way.

"Indifferentism"-- No. 2

THERE IS A frightening sentence in the seventy-sixth section of the Doctrine and Covenants. It is one which every professed follower of Christ should read and ponder.

This section tells of the varied degrees of glory in the world to come, and points out those who may be assigned to each.

In referring to the terrestrial glory it speaks of persons who have the testimony of Jesus, but who were not "valiant" in regard to it, and says:

"These are they who are not valiant in the testimony of Jesus; wherefore, they obtain not the crown over the kingdom of our God." (v. 79.)

Membership in the Church alone, then, cannot guarantee celestial glory. Neither can a "testimony of Jesus" if we are not valiant in it.

The dictionary defines the word valiant in this way: "strong and intrepid; powerful and courageous; performed with valor; bravely conducted; heroic."

Apply those expressions to the quotation above referred to in D & C 76:79 and ponder them.

The Lord has His own definitions of this teaching. To make His meaning very clear, He says:

"O ye, that embark in the service of God, see that ye serve him with all your heart, might, mind and strength, that ye may stand blameless before God at the last day." (D&C 4.)

And He adds:

"For behold, it is not meet that I should command in all things; for he that is compelled in all things, the same is a slothful and not a wise servant; wherefore he receiveth no reward.

"But he that doeth not anything until he is commanded, and receiveth a commandment with doubtful heart, and keepeth it with slothfulness, the same is damned." (D&C 58:26, 29.)

"Indifferentism," as it has been called, can rob us of our happiness here and our salvation in the world to come.

We cannot be indifferent toward the Lord and hope to receive His blessings. What parent here on earth extends himself to shower gifts upon a child who is indifferent and disobedient, and who pays no heed to the teachings of that parent?

We forget that the Gospel is a plan whereby we learn to become like God. To do so we must not only KNOW His teachings, but we must likewise DO them. But not only are we to do them, we must do them "anxiously," to use His own expression; we must do so enthusiastically, and with our whole heart, might, mind and strength.

This is what builds in us those divine attributes which make us like Him.

"Don't care" attitudes will never make us either great or successful in anything. What is as great or desirable as to see the fulfillment of the commandment: "Be ye therefore perfect, even as your Father which is in heaven is perfect"?

Such a goal requires the greatest of application and devotion. Indifferent performance can never bring it about. A "don't care" attitude will lead us in the opposite direction.

It is true that the Lord is merciful and kind, but He does not allow mercy to rob justice. It is no kindness to us to give us rewards for which we are not prepared.

The Gospel is for personal development. It is not merely a solace to our souls. The Church is His vehicle "for the perfecting of the Saints," as Paul described it, not a social institution to provide free entertainment.

Reaching heaven is strictly a matter of personal development, whereby we build into ourselves Christ-like traits of character. Being saved is not arriving at some station far off in space. It is becoming God-like in what we say and do and think.

That is the reason for God's requirement of consistency in our service to Him, for enthusiasm and "anxious" devotion. No one can be like God while being indifferent to the good things of life; no one can be considered God-like while shackled with a "don't care" attitude. Neither is it divine in any sense to give only half-hearted effort.

Ask any student if he won honors with mediocre efforts in school. Ask any general if his battles were won by "don't care" armies and indifferent officers.

Then can the greatest of all achievements — to become like God — be obtained through indifference or half-way measures?

We must be valiant in the testimony of Jesus.

The Problem Of "Drop-Outs"

IN EVERY CHURCH there are both active and inactive members. It is likewise true of our own.

Whereas most of our people love the Gospel and make an earnest effort to live it, there are many who do not and drift into other interests, some far from being wholesome.

There are many reasons for "drop-outs" in the Church. Sometimes people are offended for one cause or another, and absent themselves from further activity.

Some are lured away by unwholesome companions at school, at work or on the playground, and because of their own weakness they fall into the habits of the crowd they follow.

At times home conditions force children into the inactive ranks. Uncooperative parents can do this, as do unbelieving fathers and mothers who do not make religion an important part of the home.

Children are likely to follow the examples of their parents, and when father and mother neglect Church attendance, children do likewise; and when parents drink or smoke, the children usually adopt the same habits.

Even some fairly active parents teach habits of absence from Church by going on vacation trips over weekends, treating the Sabbath like any other holiday.

But there is still another cause for drop-outs, and that lies within the Church itself.

When Church activity is poorly handled, that very inefficiency can so disgust many of those who attend that they lose their desire ever to return.

With each drop-out from the Church a problem is created in someone's home, and Church officers and teachers may be to blame.

Unpleasant as it is to contemplate, we ourselves can cause problems in the homes of our neighbors by our mediocre performance at Church.

One of the surest ways of helping a family to strengthen its youth is to eradicate the drop-outs in the Church.

The best way we can accomplish that is to do our Church work so well that interest in our classes will be so great that those who come will not want to stay away.

That is why the Lord asks us to do our work to the best of our ability, with all our heart, might, mind and strength.

How many classes have doubled and tripled in attendance merely by the efforts of a really competent teacher? And how many classes have seen the attendance diminish when a poor teacher has taken his place?

Some well-meaning Church workers literally drive young people away, unwittingly, it is admitted, by their lack of understanding of their responsibilities, lack of patience, lack of skill in doing their work, and lack of intelligent preparation for it.

If we by our personal failure should cause distaste for Church attendance in the mind of any person, we contribute to his spiritual delinquency, and cause a problem within his home for his parents and others who love him.

We have an inspired Church program. There is no other to compare with it. But it is no more effective than the manner in which it is used and adopted in our local congregations.

Our use of this inspired program is no better than our understanding of it and our devotion in implementing it.

Every Church worker can be a savior on Mount Zion if he or she has a mind to be.

Depending upon our personal attitude, we can save our people, or we can lose them by neglect and carelessness on our part.

Every Church worker can take a significant step toward eliminating the drop-out problem by following the injunction of the scripture:

"Wherefore, now let every man learn his duty, and to act in the office in which he is appointed, in all diligence.

"He that is slothful shall not be counted worthy to stand, and he that learns not his duty and shows himself not approved shall not be counted worthy to stand." (D&C 107:99-100.)

In Or Of The Church

IN ONE OF the revelations to the Prophet Joseph Smith the Lord cautioned us saying: "Trifle not with sacred things."

This timely warning at first was given to some early members of the Church who did not fully understand the significance of the restoration of the Gospel.

But it is equally applicable to us.

Particularly are we not to trifle with the sacred name nor the divine work of Christ, as is done in insincere or hypocritical acts.

Many claim to hold membership in one church or another, but admit that they do little about it. One might say, "I am a Catholic but I am not a practicing Catholic," or another might say, "I am a Mormon but not a practicing Mormon," or likewise one might claim to be a Presbyterian but not practice the teachings of that church.

It never seems to occur to them that if they are not "practicing" Christians in the genuine sense, they are hardly Christians at all. The Savior taught that those who are not for Him are against Him. If we do not practice His teachings, can we say we are "for" Him?

What then is a Christian? Is he not one who practices the Lord's precepts in his daily life? Is he not one who earnestly strives to become Christ-like in his habits and attitudes and in his relationships with all mankind?

If a person is not a practicing Catholic, is he really a Catholic at all? If he is not a practicing "Mormon," can he in reality claim to be a genuine Latter-day Saint? Or a Presbyterian, if he ignores his creed?

This thought might be extended also to our national allegiance. If a citizen of this country is not a practicing American, is he worthy of the name? Compare the boy risking his life in Vietnam with one who has turned hippie, and ask which is the real American.

We often speak of apostasy from the Gospel. It appears in various forms, and is not found alone in those who leave one church to join another, or even among those who leave Christianity to adopt some non-Christian faith.

Every act of disobedience and rebellion against the Lord's precepts is an evidence of apostasy to that degree. To resist the Savior to any extent is apostasy on that point.

When we are baptized we take upon ourselves the name of Christ and covenant to serve Him and keep His commandments.

When we partake of the Sacrament of the Lord's Supper we do likewise, and when we accept ordination to the priesthood we agree to live by His every word.

Can we then be true Christians if we fail to keep our covenants and follow Him? Is our failure to obey not an apostasy to the extent of our disobedience? Do we not step over the line into the Devil's territory, as expressed by President George Albert Smith, whenever we refuse to obey the Lord?

The true Christian will learn the truth about the Lord and His Church, and will willingly take His yoke upon him. No one can be a true Christian without learning His truth. We must have an intelligent faith, for no one can be saved in ignorance. God cannot be considered incomprehensible, otherwise how could we worship Him? Therefore we must learn the facts about Christ, and then adopt them. No substitute will do. He has but one way, one Church, one faith, one baptism, one plan of life.

Even though we already have found the right way, if we fail to keep the commandments we still jeopardize our salvation.

One may be IN the Church but not OF the Church, as truly as he may be in the world but not of the world.

Church membership alone will not save. If one is IN the Church he must also make himself OF the Church by his active participation in its program.

We trifle with sacred things if we profess devotion but resist our responsibilities, and except we repent, we may reap the whirlwind.

Call For An Awakening

MODERN DENOMINATIONAL CHRISTIANITY must do two things:

1. The churches must concern themselves more with basic Christian doctrine and less with devising gimmicks to court the attention of elusive modern man.

2. They must stop hating their neighbors all week and then on Sunday "receive the sacrament of love, for only a 'phony' Christian would do that."

Such were the comments of some leading clergymen as quoted recently by the Associated Press.

"Nominal Christianity has had it," was the stark assessment of present-day church life voiced by a leading Methodist theologian, the Reverend Dr. Albert Outler. Others have sounded similar views.

They call for firmer commitment to basic doctrine and its demands, and they challenge what they consider a rash of lax departures from it to appeal to passing, modern outlooks.

"The time may have come for theology to be more concerned with the truth of the Christian faith than with courting the elusive modern man," says the Reverend Dr. William Hordern, a United Church of Canada scholar.

There also is a growing conclusion that the churches are entering a period when their character and makeup will require tougher dedication to gospel teaching, in an atmosphere of much disbelief.

"In the new era — and it has started already — phony Christians will be recognized as phony," Roman Catholic Archbishop Robert E. Lucey of San Antonio told a recent gathering there.

In this connection, two tendencies, cited as widespread problems in recent church life, have drawn increasing fire from various religious leaders, said the Associated Press. They are:

1. The casual apathy of many churchgoers toward doctrine and its implications for conduct. This indifference, and vagueness about specific belief, has been brought out in numerous studies.

2. The recent "splurge" of novel, iconoclastic approaches to faith often by some theologians themselves, such as the coiners of the "Death of God" label for the modern technological age. Both approaches, said the news dispatch, are producing a backlash, with signs of a counter trend, resisting the casual, complacent type of churchmanship and the scaling down of doctrinal criteria.

Noting the flurry of assaults on classic Christian beliefs, the Reverend Dr. Eugene Carson Blake, general secretary of the World Council of Churches, told its central committee meeting in August on the island of Crete that the interdenominational body must stick to gospel standards, the Associated Press concluded.

A return to the true doctrines of Christ would be the salvation of Christianity and the world, for not only would mankind then worship Him in spirit and in truth, but they would put aside all hypocrisy and begin to love their neighbors as themselves.

But to return to true Christian doctrine would mean to abandon man-made doctrines, for man's uninspired ways and teachings are not God's.

Man-made creeds would have to go.

Denominationalism would of necessity come to an end, for Christ is not divided. We cannot be "some of Paul, some of Apollos, some of Peter, and some of Christ." True Christianity demands unity.

The rejection of current revelation and modern prophets would have to end also and everyone would of necessity look for new modern revelation, since God will do nothing "but he revealeth his secret unto his servants the prophets."

How far will modern Christians go in a return to Christ? All the way?

Or will their hearts still yearn for their man-made traditions and their widespread free-thinking denominationalism, as the followers of Moses yearned for the flesh pots of Egypt?

Ancient Israel was kept out of the Promised Land for their failure to accept the whole plan of God.

Will the denominations of today follow a similar pattern?